CHRISTIANITY IN
3D

LARRY HART

TruthAflame
—PRESS—

TRUTHAFLAME
——PRESS——

Christianity in 3D

Copyright © 2014 by Larry Hart

Cover design and interior design: Kevin Hart

truthaflamepress.com

TABLE OF CONTENTS

INTRODUCTION

3D is all the rage! Movies, television, and electronic gaming will never be the same. People are already demanding the change. And we are way ahead of the red-and-blue cardboard glasses of yesteryear. Whether we're pursuing entertainment at the movie theater or at home, we want that third dimension. It adds realism and immediacy. *Avatar* was dazzling in 3D IMAX. But we want to be able to cart it home as well. Now we can! 3D is just better when it comes to experiencing the full impact of a movie or game. Entertainment is better in 3D. *Life* is better in 3D as well—that is, real life, the life that is offered us in the Good News of Jesus Christ.

Unfortunately, the vision of too many Christians is fuzzy when it comes to Christianity in 3D. Too often they are stuck in a two-dimensional "flat" world of a so-called Christian life without full meaning, purpose, and reality. Haunted with the sense that there must be more to authentic Christianity than a desultory drifting through life—believing the right things and behaving the right ways, but lacking a passion and purpose in life—many believers today need to discover new dimensions to their faith. They are longing for Christianity in 3D!

> Lacking a passion and purpose in life— many believers today need to discover new dimensions to their faith.

The one essential piece of equipment to the enjoyment of 3D is the appropriate pair of glasses. Early on, I just had to sample 3D television at the electronics store. As I walked toward the enormous flat-screen television, I was immediately aware of how blurred the picture was. I noticed three pairs of glasses by the convenient theater chairs, so I selected a pair, took a seat, and put on the glasses—still blurred. The sales person pointed out that the glasses had to be turned on themselves. And when I did—wow!—a whole new world of television leaped off the screen at me. I returned home to my wife and announced that we simply had to keep up with latest technology if we were going to be effective Christians in the twenty-first century. Encumbered with a strong sense of realism and financial responsibility, my wife begged to differ. I soon acceded to her wisdom. But I also learned a lesson about 3D Christianity: You have to have the right glasses.

And what exactly would those be? John Calvin told us centuries ago the answer to that question. He said we need the Bible as "spectacles" to see and appreciate fully God's revelation in his creation. Of course, this principle extends to the New Testament gospel as well. And the central focus of all the Scriptures is Jesus Christ. Without a thorough knowledge of Scripture and a personal, growing knowledge of Jesus, then, life will always be a little out of focus—even for Christians. But with this knowledge all kinds of vistas open up to us!

But precisely how do we go about obtaining this knowledge of the Scriptures (the Written Word) and Jesus (the Incarnate Word). First and foremost, we need the help of the Holy Spirit. Indeed, we will find what the Reformers always taught, that the Word and the Spirit work in tandem. And this activity does not take place in a vacuum. *We need each other in this quest!* That is, we need the *church*. We need the Spirit, the Scriptures, and the Saints: The Scriptures provide the objective norm of our faith. The Spirit—who gave us these Scriptures—illuminates our understanding of them. And the saints help each other appropriate and live out these saving, transforming truths. In this way we become better followers of Christ.

3D works when the perspectives of our two eyes are correlated to provide a more complete picture. Each of our eyes provides data which the brain coordinates into a perception of both depth and velocity. Unfortunate souls who lose the sight of one eye can readily document this process: Judging depth and velocity becomes a daunting task until the brain readjusts. Having two perspectives on reality makes

> We need the Spirit, the Scriptures, and the Saints.

all the difference! Hegel developed a complete philosophy on this insight with his treatment of thesis, antithesis, and synthesis. And have you ever noticed how many of the most important teachings of our faith are "two-eyed" truths? We are required to hold together and to integrate two truths or perspectives in order to grasp the nature of the reality we are exploring.

God, for example, is both three and one. Christ is both divine and human. God is sovereign, yet we are responsible. If we fail to integrate the two perspectives, we end up compromising the truth. Failure to apprehend a dimension that is really there is fatal when it comes to our quest for truth. Western societies are clearly suffering from a massive loss of transcendence—that there really is something out there beyond our five senses. But when we become aware of another dimension, our potential for recovering meaning and beauty increases exponentially.

I'm convinced that believers in America need to discover afresh the three fundamental dimensions of Christianity. Anybody who knows anything at all about the present state of the American churches would say we need to discover *something*. Decline is the norm. Belief is waning in many quarters. Our culture is disintegrating before our very eyes. And Christians seem to be light years away from being the salt and light to society that Jesus taught about. We need 3D! We need a full dose of the faith and not merely an inoculation. We need to examine afresh three foundational truths: (1) who God is; (2) what God wants to do *in* our lives; and (3) what God wants to do *through* our lives..

Who is God? Who am I? John Calvin began his *Institutes* reminding us that these two questions are inseparable and, rightly answered, lead to true wisdom. But who is God? Theologians tell us that fully answering that query necessitates exploring God's essence, names, attributes, and triunity. In the process, we are literally engulfed with Christianity in 3D, the blindingly brilliant light of the revelation of a triune God—Father, Son, and Holy Spirit! Not just a 3D God, but a God of *infinite* dimensions!

But what does God want to do in our lives? This question assumes the biblical perspectives on who we are as persons created by God, for God, and in his image. We literally exist for the glory of God—or were intended to do so. But something went wrong. Theologians call it the Fall. It is not a mere mythology or theory; it is a tragic reality. And God has set about to address the situation. This saving work of God has three fundamental dimensions: Paschal, Purifying, and Pentecostal. In each of these dimensions, the Holy Spirit applies what the Father has done for us through the Son: He has come on a rescue mission to make us into a new creation, to transform our lives daily, and empower our mission and ministry in life. This is how God wants to work *in* us. But how does he want to work *through* us as his people corporately?

Jesus himself set the pace for us in his own earthly ministry. Twice Matthew described Jesus' earthly ministry in 3D fashion, telling us how Jesus went about "teaching in their synagogues, preaching the good news of the kingdom, and healing every disease and sickness" (Matt. 4:23/ 9:35 NIV1984). As the Body of Christ, shouldn't the ministry of the church also be seen in this threefold (3D) fashion? We will need to explore the implications of this revolutionary truth!

Three-dimensional Christianity is the most powerful force on the planet. The Bible calls it the very *kingdom of God*! It is God showing up and shaking everything up. It is disruptive and disconcerting. It simply cannot be ignored. It is in your face. It is friendly but also fierce. It is also fun! It is a party, a celebration. At the same time, it carries a sense of profound concern and urgency. It weeps for the sins and sicknesses of humanity. It cries out to God for transformation. It can settle for nothing less than the rightful rule of God on the planet he

> Three-dimensional Christianity is the most powerful force on the planet...the very *kingdom of God!*

made, owns, and loves. So pick up a pair of glasses and join the throng of believers who have discovered 3D Christianity. It is a Christianity worthy of our whole lives. Nothing else can give this kind of meaning to life. And it all starts with Jesus. It is all about who he is and what he did. And only the Father can reveal the fullness of this reality to us by his Spirit. Let's get started!

WHO
GOD IS

CHAPTER ONE
FATHER

The midday Mediterranean sun beat down on the brow of a tired, thirsty Jesus. He sat by Jacob's well in Sychar. Most often, people would come to draw water from the well at early morning or late evening. But now a woman arrives at the well to draw water by herself. What Jesus does next is simply unthinkable: He, a single Jewish man and spiritual leader, addresses this Samaritan woman of questionable character and asks her for a drink of water. The conversation that ensues is one of the most remarkable recorded interviews of Jesus' ministry.

> The Samaritan woman said to him, "You are a Jew and I am a Samaritan woman. How can you ask me for a drink?" (For Jews do not associate with Samaritans.)
> Jesus answered her, "If you knew the gift of God and who it is that asks you for a drink, you would have asked him and he would have given you living water (John 4:9–10).

Jesus went on to inform the woman that the gift of God, the living water, he was offering the woman would become in her "a spring of water welling up to eternal life" (v. 14).

When the woman asks Jesus to give her this water, Jesus tells her to get her husband and come back. Knowing that she has had five husbands and that the man with whom she now lives is not her husband, Jesus confronts her sin problem. And typical of us sinners (and that's *all* of us), the woman throws up the smokescreen of the worship controversy between Jews and Samaritans. Jesus' rejoinder gets to the heart of the matter and also contains one of the most important revelations in the Bible on who God is and what it truly means to know and worship him. True worshipers, Jesus said, "will worship the Father in the Spirit and in truth" (v. 23). "God is spirit, and his worshipers must worship in the Spirit and in truth" (v. 24).

> What too often goes unnoticed is the simple statement, "God is spirit."

Jesus said that true worshipers will worship *the Father*. This was a distinctive emphasis of all that Jesus said and did. He was all about the Father! He claimed a unique relationship of intimacy with the Father. He offered us intimacy with the Father as well by our becoming followers of Jesus himself. He explained that this kind of a worshipful life was only possible through the help of the Holy Spirit. The singularly *spiritual* nature of our knowledge and worship of God is obvious here. What too often goes unnoticed is the simple statement, "God is spirit."

In fact, John's writings contain three of the most important programmatic statements on who God is to be found in all of the Bible: (1) "God is spirit" (John 4:24); (2) "God is light" (1 John 1:5); and (3) "God is love" (1 John 4:8, 16). God's spiritual essence is contained in the first statement and the majestic properties of his holy/loving attributes are contained in the latter two statements. But what does it mean to say that God is spirit?

God Is Spirit

Theologians have pondered those three simple words for centuries and have developed a pretty sophisticated terminology to unlock their theological significance. Further, we have in this memorable story a clear revelation of the most important Christian name for God: "Father, Son, and Holy Spirit." And this revelation is a *saving* revelation. As the people to whom the Samaritan woman had witnessed said, "we know that this man really is the Savior of the world" (v. 42). In other words, as Jesus brought his saving message to the Samaritan woman he was also revealing who God is and what it truly means to know and love him. This is truly 3D Christianity—a multi-dimensional God communicating a multi-dimensional salvation! This is Good News; there is no better news.

God as spirit is not limited to a physical body as we are. Theologians utilize technical terms such as aseity, simplicity, immanence, transcendence, and the like to unwrap this concept. First, as spirit God is *a se*—"of himself," i.e., self-causing. When someone asks, "If God made everything, then who made God?" they have failed to grasp God's aseity. God is the only being who causes himself to exist. Philosophical theologian Paul Tillich liked to refer to God as Being itself, from which our existence is derived. Tillich's own conceptions in this regard were found by many to be defective, but his idea of God's own self-existence as being causative of all that exists was valid. In other words, we *exist*, God *is*. That little proposition, "God is," contains within itself just about everything the Bible has to say about who God is. Theologian Carl Henry said it best:

> If we give the subject "God" and the predicate "is" their true and full sense, we must speak of God's essence, names, attributes, and triunity, and do so expressly on the basis of his revelatory self-disclosure addressed to his created and fallen creatures.[1]

---

1 Carl F. H. Henry, *God, Revelation and Authority, Vol. V* (Dallas: Word, 1982), p. 131.

Henry provides us with a summary outline of the biblical doctrine of God: (1) essence; (2) names; (3) attributes; and (4) triunity. We have looked at the aseity of God. But what is meant by his *simplicity*?

God's simplicity refers to his not being comprised of "parts." He is undivided; he is indivisible. He is complete and unified in all that he is, says, and does. He is not partly loving and partly holy. As a triune God, he is not comprised of a collection of finite, independently existing persons—a committee-God, so to speak. His attributes describe all that he is throughout his entire being. Thus, in dealing with the sins of fallen humanity he can manifest both wrath and mercy in non-contradictory ways. God's simplicity as spirit sets him apart completely from all that he has made. This insight leads us to two of the most important dimensions of God's essence: immanence and transcendence.

When Stan Grenz and Roger Olson set themselves to the task of writing a survey of twentieth-century theology, their first challenge was precisely how to get a handle on the task. The concepts of immanence and transcendence became key to their analysis, the best way both to contrast and evaluate all the persons and schools of thought they surveyed.[2] God's immanence and transcendence, perhaps more than any other concepts, convey to us the essence of God as spirit in relation to his creation. God as spirit is immanent— i.e., everywhere present throughout the created order. Scientists have helped us to discover the vastness of the universe. And it is truly mind boggling to realize that God is present to his creation throughout the vast reaches of space.

I once saw a sign on the back of a city bus advertising their city-wide service with the declaration, "We are ubiquitous!" meaning you could find a bus anywhere in town. God is ubiquitous! The psalmist asked, "Where can I go from your Spirit? Where can I flee from your presence?"

---

2 Stanley J. Grenz and Roger E. Olson, *Twentieth-Century Theology: God and the World in a Transitional Age* (Downers Grove, Ill.: InterVarsity Press, 1992).

(Psalm 139: 7). In terms of our little planet alone, there is no place you can go to escape God's presence. God is immanent not only in relation to space. He is also immanent in relation to time. He is our traveling partner through time. History is really *his* story. Moses prayed, "Lord, you have been our dwelling place throughout all generations" (Psalm 90:1). But God's immanence is incomplete without his transcendence.

God's transcendence refers to his being wholly other than, outside of, and independent from all that he has made. As the popular saying goes in some Christian circles, "God is God and you're not!" That saying is absolutely true and very important in our day. To say God is transcendent is to say that he is set apart from us—he is *holy*. In western cultures especially, this aspect of God's essence has been largely compromised. We tend either to lose God in his creation (pantheism, eastern religions, new age teachings) or allow him to be eclipsed by the material realm (naturalism, secularism, atheism). The worldview of *Avatar* is an illustration of the former. The writings of Richard Dawkins would represent the latter point of view. And for Christians, keeping the balance between immanence and transcendence is crucial.

For some, God is their immanent "pal." He is the object of a warm and fuzzy faith in which God exists as the "great need-meet-er," a heavenly vending machine, whose purpose is to "keep me happy." We will learn later that God does have a disposition to promote our happiness. But we must never forget his transcendence. He is our sovereign creator God. And we exist for his glory and pleasure, not the other way around. Ultimately, what matters is not whether we're happy, but whether he's happy. In other words, we can be shocked at the total loss of transcendence in atheism, but be suffering a similar loss in our own personally constructed God.

Sometimes when I hear a person say, "*My* God is not like that (a holy God of judgment, for example), I want to respond, "Well, maybe *your* God, the one you have constructed out of your own imagination, doesn't really exist!" Too often today we begin with ourselves—our own reason and experience—rather than with divine revelation. Remember, those "glasses" are crucial to accurately perceiving God and reality as they really are: in other words, 3D Christianity.

So far, we have been looking primarily at John's first statement, "God is spirit" (John 4:24). To get the full biblical revelation of who God is we will need to examine his other two three-word summaries: "God is light" (1 John 1:5); and "God is love" (1 John 4:8, 16). We are getting at the heart of the essence of God when we say that he is *holy love*. He is holy (God is light) and he is infinite love (God is love).

God Is Light

The apostle John wrote these simple, yet profound and memorable, words:

> This is the message we have heard from him and declare to you: God is light; in him there is no darkness at all. If we claim to have fellowship with him and yet walk in the darkness, we lie and do not live out the truth. But if we walk in the light, as he is in the light, we have fellowship with one another, and the blood of Jesus, his Son, purifies us from all sin (1 John 1:5–7).

This portrayal of God is a far cry from the "god" of *Star Wars*, who is a "force" with a dark side (represented by Darth Vader) and a light side (represented by Luke Skywalker). In fact, what we learn from John in this paragraph can transform our lives: God is *light*! There is no darkness in him at all. The implications of this truth are far reaching. It is truly good news.

Yes, God is a mystery. Yes, we will never be able to fully fathom him (even in eternity). Yes, his triune nature busts wide open all our linear, logical categories. It truly is a mystery we are dealing with here. But it is a mystery of *light*! We will never discover a sinister, capricious side to God. There is none. We will never find a peeved potentate, an egomaniacal clown, a selfish, self-absorbed deity who truly cares for nothing and no one but himself. Notice, all these negative depictions would apply best to the *devil*! The devil has always wanted to usurp God's position, and he has influenced fallen humanity in that direction as well.

God is light. He is the epitome of all that is good and right and true. He is the perfection of beauty. He is the highest joy, the most desirable of all beings. He is the very meaning of the universe: He is its source, guide, and goal (Rom. 11:36). He is the ultimate standard for truth, ethics, morals, meaning, purpose, and beauty. The reason we *have* reason is because of him (compare John 1:9). Nietzsche was right when he argued that there are only two possible choices in life, faith in God or nihilism. Unfortunately, he chose the latter and went mad—as are western societies today, it seems, and for the same basic reason. John reminds us of this proclivity in all people as he comments on God's purposeful sending of his Son into history: "This is the verdict: Light has come into the world, but people loved darkness instead of light because their deeds were evil" (John 3:19).

To say God is light is to say God is holy. And there are many properties of that holiness. He is a God of wrath, righteousness, power, constancy, eternity, glory, and wisdom.[3] Notice, I mention wrath first. It is perhaps the most troublesome property of God's holiness. Some theologians even reject it as descriptive of God. And yet, in another sense we would be scandalized if God did *not* exhibit this attribute. Who among us does not recoil at the rampant cruelty and injustices across the globe? Surely it is right to express righteous

---

3 See my treatment of these in *Truth Aflame: Theology for the Church in Renewal* (Grand Rapids: Zondervan, 2005), 88-100.

indignation—wrath!—in response to these unspeakable atrocities and intransigent animosities. We would be less than human not to do so. How much more a holy, loving God who treasures every person on this earth with an infinite love and affection! The question is, why doesn't he do something about all this rampant evil? That was precisely the question of the prophet Habakkuk.

Habakkuk lived in times quite similar to our own. Empires were shifting. Political unrest, economic decline, violence, a compromised religious system, and blatant paganism were the norm. Even God's people in Judah were participating in the iniquities of their age. Seeing the Babylonian invasion on the horizon, Habakkuk's complaints to God were understandable. Why does God tolerate this mess? How long will it be before he does something about it? How could he even consider using an even more pagan nation to judge Judah? Habakkuk was looking for mercy in a day filled with wrath.

The book he wrote beautifully depicts his journey from fear to faith. He starts with more questions than answers and ends with a confident faith that the God who truly does judge nations and shows wrath against the destructive sins of humanity is also the God of infinite love and mercy. Habakkuk's lyrical prayer, which culminates his book (ch. 3), expresses this faith beautifully. He begins with this petition: "Lord, I have heard of your fame; I stand in awe of your deeds, Lord. Repeat them in our day, in our time make them known; in wrath remember mercy" (Hab. 3:2). *In wrath remember mercy.* Habakkuk saw no contradiction here. In this song he both celebrates God's wrath and rejoices in God's righteous salvation.

Isaiah's later prophecies flesh out precisely how God would sovereignly restore Jerusalem to Judah: He would use Cyrus of Persia himself! The Lord belittles the lifeless idols of the day and announces the good news in beautiful words of comfort and promise:

You heavens above, rain down my righteousness;
    let the clouds shower it down.
Let the earth open wide,
    let salvation spring up,
let righteousness flourish with it;
    I, the LORD, have created it (Isa. 45:8).

Notice the correlation of righteousness and salvation. The Lord goes on to say, "I will raise up Cyrus in my righteousness: I will make all his ways straight. He will rebuild my city and set my exiles free" (v. 13). Then God reminds Judah that he, not the wooden idols of the pagans, would deliver them, and he alone could tell them beforehand what was going to happen:

Who foretold this long ago,
    who declared it from the distant past?
Was it not I, the LORD?
    And there is no God apart from me,
a righteous God and a Savior;
    there is none but me. (v. 21).

A righteous God and a Savior: Only the sovereign, all-powerful God, who is really there, as Francis Schaeffer would say, could do such a thing! This leads us then to the third property of God's holiness: power.

The Greek philosopher Parmenides, more than four centuries before Christ, asked one of the most profound and important questions: Why is there something and not nothing? In our day we might couch the question, Why did the Big Bang happen—and how? The biblical answer is, of course, that God simply spoke the universe into existence, making something out of nothing. That's power! Further, this vast universe could be, the scientists tell us, only one of an infinite number of universes! We're still trying to find these things out and fathom them. As Jeremiah said, "Ah, Sovereign LORD, you have made the heavens and the earth by your great power and outstretched arm. Nothing is too hard for you" (Jer. 32:17). But beyond creation we see God's power in our redemption.

The biblical accounts of the central events in redemptive history—the Exodus in the Hebrew Scriptures and Easter in the New Testament—clearly demonstrate the power of God. Only God could part a sea. Only God could resurrect Jesus. The gospel itself "is the power of God that brings salvation to everyone who believes" (Rom. 1:16). "The message of the cross," Paul told the Corinthians, "is the power of God" (1 Cor. 1:18). Only God can transform a person's life. Peter celebrates this reality with these exultant words: "Blessed be the God and Father of our Lord Jesus Christ! According to his great mercy, he has caused us to be born again to a living hope through the resurrection of Jesus Christ from the dead" (1 Peter 1:3 ESV). Thus, in both creation and redemption, God is revealed as a God of infinite power. Further, our all-powerful Creator and Redeemer is faithful, trustworthy, and dependable. He is constant; he doesn't change.

The one constant of our own lives is change. Everything and everyone change. But not so with God: "I the LORD do not change" (Mal 3:6). The whole universe is in constant change, and God has inundated us with blessings both within it and beyond it. And "these good gifts come down from the Creator of the sun, moon, and stars, who does not change like their shifting shadows" (James 1:17 NCV). At the same time, we must not take God's constancy to mean that he is static and impersonal. He has chosen freely to interact with us in space, time, and history. In that sense he does "change" in his attitudes (Gen. 6:6, 7; Jer. 3:12; Isa. 54:8; 64:7) and actions (Amos 7:3, 6; Jer. 42:10; 1 Sam. 15:35). But he never changes in his character (Num. 23:19; Ps. 102:27 Mal. 3:6; James 1:17) or counsel (Ps. 33:11; Heb. 6:17).

The universe wears out like a garment: "But you [God] remain the same, and your years will never end" (Ps. 102:26–27). Thus, our constant

God is also the *eternal* God. He is before time (Ps. 90:2), above time (Isa. 57:15), and ahead of time (Rom. 15:13). Our eternal God can do two things at once: He can see time in its totality as a completed reality and also interact with us throughout time. Obviously, only he could pull that off! God can do both of these things simultaneously because he is both immanent and transcendent. And the immanent disclosure of his transcendent holiness is what we call his *glory*.

God's glory is his manifested presence. It is his self-revelation. And "the whole earth is full of his glory" (Isa. 6:3). "The heavens declare the glory of God" as well (Ps. 19:1). Thus, God's glory also points to his omnipresence. Sin has blinded us to this radiance of God's majesty. Were we to be given direct access to it in our present state, it would destroy us. But one day, the Bible promises us, "the earth will be filled with the knowledge of the glory of the LORD as the waters cover the sea" (Hab. 2:14).

The Lord made his glory accessible to us in the Incarnation: "The Word became flesh and made his dwelling among us. We have seen his glory, the glory of the one and only Son, who came from the Father, full of grace and truth" (John 1:14). The words "made his dwelling among us" could be translated "tabernacled among us," alluding to the *Shekinah* glory which shined in the pillar of cloud and fire (Ex. 13:21–22), at Sinai (19:16–25), and most importantly in the tabernacle itself (Ex. 40:34–38). Jesus once prayed for us, "Father, I want those you have given me to be with me where I am, and to see my glory, the glory you have given me because you loved me before the creation of the world" (John 17:24). And that request will be granted! God not only gave us access to his glory in Jesus; he also gave us his wisdom.

For believers, Jesus Christ has become "wisdom from God—that is, our righteousness, holiness and redemption" (1 Cor. 1:30). The message of Christ crucified may seem scandalous to Jews and moronic to Gentiles, but to us whom God has called, Christ is "the power of God and the wisdom of God" (1 Cor. 1:23–24). Psalm 104 celebrates our Creator God and his manifold works: "How many are your works,

LORD! In wisdom you made them all" (Ps. 104:24). There are whole books of the Bible dedicated to divine wisdom, wisdom literature such as Job, Proverbs, and Ecclesiastes. But the Scriptures continually return to Christ himself as the focal point, Christ "in whom are hidden all the treasures of wisdom and knowledge" (Col. 2:3).

So God is light. He is a holy God of wrath, righteousness, power, constancy, eternity, glory, and wisdom. But the culmination of the revealed attributes of God comes with John's words, "God is love" (1 John 4:8, 16). In Jesus and his cross we have the greatest revelation of the heart of the Father—a God of mercy, grace, patience, kindness, faithfulness, goodness, and knowledge.[4]

God is Love

God is love—not "God is loving" or "love is God." God's very essence is love, and we should derive our understanding of love from him. We define love from God, not God from love. And what is love? "This is love: not that we loved God, but that he loved us and sent his Son as an atoning sacrifice for our sins" (1 John 4:10). How has God shown us his love? "This is how God showed his love among us: He sent his one and only Son into the world that we might live through him" (1 John 4:9). "For God so loved the world that he gave his one and only Son, that whoever believes in him shall not perish but have eternal life" (John 3:16). In other words, we should turn to Jesus to find God's love. We should look at the cross. At the cross we discover a God of infinite mercy, grace, patience, kindness, faithfulness, goodness, and loving knowledge of us.

> God's very essence is love, and we should derive our understanding of love from him.

---

4 Again, for a more detailed treatment of these attributes see my *Truth Aflame*, 100-119.

First, we must make note of the Father's mercy. Christians rejoice continually in his great mercy. "Blessed be the God and Father of our Lord Jesus Christ! By his great mercy he has given us a new birth into a living hope through the resurrection of Jesus Christ from the dead (1 Peter 1:3 NRSV). In the Bible, "the mercy of God is always a picture of the condition of man on the one hand and of the compassion of God on the other."[5] The apostle Paul gave poignant depiction of our miserable, sinful plight and God's merciful saving power with these words:

> Once you were dead because of your disobedience and your many sins. You used to live in sin, just like the rest of the world, obeying the devil—the commander of the powers in the unseen world. . . .
>
> But God is so rich in mercy, and he loved us so much, that even though we were dead because of our sins, he gave us life when he raised Christ from the dead. (It is only by God's grace that you have been saved!) (Ephesians 2:1–4 NLT).

Like the rest of humankind, Paul reminds us, "we were by nature deserving of wrath," but God "is rich in mercy" (Eph. 2:3–4). Israel was continually unfaithful to God. "Yet he was merciful; he forgave their iniquities and did not destroy them. Time after time he restrained his anger and did not stir up his full wrath" (Ps. 78:38). Just as Hosea took back his unfaithful wife Gomer, so God promised to restore Israel: "And I will take you for my wife forever; I will take you for my wife in righteousness and in justice, in steadfast love, and in mercy" (Hosea 2:19 NRSV). We have a sympathetic high priest in Jesus, the writer of Hebrews reminds us—a high priest "who has been tempted in every way, just as we are—yet he did not sin" (Heb. 4:15). Therefore, we can "approach God's throne of grace with confidence, so that we

---

5 Dale Moody, *The Word of Truth* (Grand Rapids: Eerdmans, 1981), 105.

may receive mercy and find grace to help us in our time of need" (v. 16). It is a *throne* we are approaching, so we come with reverence toward a sovereign, holy God. But it is a throne of *grace*, so we can also come before him boldly and freely, with assurance and confidence. It is a throne of grace, and that grace is the leitmotif of the Christian symphony!

C. S. Lewis once came in late to a conversation among comparative religion scholars concerning the uniqueness of Christianity. Having learned the question, he responded immediately, "Oh, that's easy. It's grace."[6] Lewis himself had already been conquered by this mysterious divine grace, moving out of atheism to become one of the greatest advocates of the gospel. Grace is the essence of the gospel. And it is what sets Christianity apart from all other religions and ideologies. I teach an entire course each year in seminary on this topic, and it has been one of the richest experiences of my life.

In my studies I have discovered three fundamental biblical truths concerning grace: First, grace is *an attribute* of God. It describes how he inundates fallen humanity with his undeserved love. Second, it is a term the Bible uses to point to God's saving *action* on our behalf. It is God's powerful love reaching down to rescue us! And third, it points to an *attitude* God's people are to exhibit toward each other and all others. In a nutshell, the Father reaches down to us with his "two hands" (as Irenaeus would put it), the Son and the Spirit, creating the universe, governing and preserving his creation, and redeeming fallen humanity. Thomas C. Oden provides these helpful summary comments:

> Grace is an overarching term for all God's gifts to humanity, all
> the blessings of salvation, all events through which are manifested

---

6 See Scott Hoezee, *The Riddle of Grace* (Grand Rapids: Eerdmans, 1996), 41–42 and Philip Yancey, *What's So Amazing About Grace?* (Grand Rapids: Zondervan, 1997), 45.

God's own self-giving. Grace is a divine attribute revealing the heart of the one God, the premise of all spiritual blessing.

Grace is the favor shown by God to sinners. It is the divine goodwill offered to those who neither inherently deserve nor can ever hope to earn it. It is the divine disposition to work in our hearts, wills, and actions, so as actively to communicate God's self-giving love for humanity.[7]

Our gracious God is also *patient*. He has held back his power to judge fallen humanity: "Instead he is patient with you, not wanting anyone to perish, but everyone to come to repentance" (2 Peter 3:9; see also Rom 2:4). The Lord is a "compassionate and gracious God, slow to anger, abounding in love and faithfulness" (Ex. 34:6). God's *agape* love "is patient" (*makrothymeo*; Gal. 5:22), that is, it "suffers long" with us. We see in God's willingness to be patient with us his *passion* for us. The whole book of Hosea is witness to this: "Hosea is one of the most emotional books in the Bible, an outpouring of suffering love from God's heart," as Philip Yancey observes.[8]

Hosea's wife was unfaithful, but our Sovereign God is always *faithful*. "If we are faithless, he remains faithful" (2 Tim. 2:13). "If we confess our sins, He is faithful and righteous to forgive us our sins and to cleanse us from all unrighteousness" (1 John 1:9 HCSB). "God, who has called you to share everything with his Son, Jesus Christ our Lord, is faithful" (1 Cor. 1:9 NCV). People will always disappoint us. They will inevitably let us down at some point. But we can always count on God. He is loyal. He is faithful. He is a *good* God—totally good, totally trustworthy.

When Moses said to the Lord, "Now show me your glory," the Lord responded, "I will cause all my goodness to pass in front of you" (Ex. 33:18–19). Jesus said, "No one is good—except God alone" (Mk 10:18).

---

7   Thomas C. Oden, *The Transforming Power of Grace* (Nashville: Abingdon Press, 1993), 33, 206.

8   Philip Yancey, *A Guided Tour of the Bible* (Grand Rapids: Zondervan, 1989), 138.

Every truly good thing in our lives comes from God: "Every good and perfect gift is from above, coming down from the Father of the heavenly lights, who does not change like shifting shadows" (James 1:17). My earthly father sacrificed much in order to provide the best things in life for me. How much more my heavenly Father! "Taste and see that the LORD is good" (Ps. 34:8)!

Goodness in Scripture indicates generosity, benevolence, and the inclination to promote another's happiness. It describes a genuine, wholesome person to whom it is easy for one to relate. Oral Roberts was theologically astute when he continually reminded us that "God is a good God." Here is how J. I. Packer would summarize it:

> Generosity expresses the simple wish that others should have what they need to make them happy. Generosity is, so to speak, the focal point of God's moral perfection; it is the quality which determines how all God's other excellences are to be displayed.[9]

Jesus both embodied and taught this divine benevolence. And in the Sermon on the Mount he laid out this challenge: "If you then, who are evil, know how to give good gifts to your children, how much more will your Father in heaven give good things to those who ask him!" (Matt. 7:11 NRSV). Earlier in this same sermon, Jesus taught us much about the final property of God's love we will consider—his *knowledge*.

Jesus assured his disciples that they need never be anxious about the basic needs of life because "indeed your heavenly Father knows that you need all these things" (Matt. 6:32 NRSV). "And even the very hairs of your head are all numbered," he reminded them in another context. We don't need to pile up anxious words in our prayers because "your heavenly Father knows what you need before you ask him" (Matt. 6:8).

---

9   J. I. Packer, *Knowing God* (Downers Grove, Ill.: InterVarsity Press, 1973), 146–47.

David celebrated this personal, infinite, loving knowledge of God in Psalm 139. God is not some cosmic computer, but rather a loving heavenly Father who cares for his creation. Because there are no limits to his wisdom, knowledge, power, and love, he is more than able to take care of us.

This is the God of holy love whom we serve. When God stood poised to consume his people at Sinai, Moses interceded, pleading for God's continued presence (Ex. 33–34). One might display the profound revelation that ensued (Ex 34:6) as follows:

The LORD, the LORD,
  a God merciful   (1) *mercy*
  and gracious,   (2) *grace*
  slow to anger,   (3) *patience*
  and abounding in
    steadfast love   (4) *kindness*
  and faithfulness   (5) *faithfulness*

Notice that five of the seven properties of God's love (only goodness and knowledge are lacking) are contained in these words! God had said, "I will cause all My goodness to pass in front of you, and I will proclaim the name Yahweh before you" (Ex. 33:19 HCSB). In other words, God gave a revelation of his divine *attributes* by a proclamation of his holy covenant *name*, Yahweh.

When we are getting to know someone, the first thing we want to know is their name. Moses wanted to know God more intimately; he wanted to see God's glory. And God proclaimed his covenant name, Yahweh, to Moses. Earlier, when God first called Moses to rescue the people of Israel, Moses asked what he should tell the people if they inquired as to the name of the one who sent him. God replied, "I AM WHO I AM. Say this to the people of Israel: I AM has sent me to you." Then God added, "Yahweh, the God of your ancestors—the God of Abraham, the God of Isaac, and the God of Jacob—has sent me to you. This is my eternal name, my name to remember for all generations" (Ex. 3:14–15 NLT). God is! Yahweh means "he who is." God simply names himself as the self-existing one, I AM! Late, in John's gospel, Jesus will assume this same name! The New Testament witness to Jesus is that the God of Abraham, Isaac, and Jacob is the Father of our Lord Jesus Christ. Further, Jesus is revealed as Yahweh himself—Incarnate!

The study of the revealed names of God in the Scriptures is one of the most rewarding aspects of studying the doctrine of God. For our purposes here, the most important name for our consideration is the name *Father*. Jesus himself put the accent on this name when he revealed his unique relationship with the Father as Abba (Mark 14:36) and when he offered us the opportunity to call God our own Father through faith in Jesus. Through the indwelling of the Holy Spirit, all true believers find themselves crying out "Abba, Father"! Knowing God as Father is the greatest privilege of the believer.

Thomas A. Smail pointed out that we have had a Jesus movement and a charismatic movement with its emphasis on the Holy Spirit but that Christianity is really a Father movement.[10] As the apostle Paul would put it, when affirming the unity of Jew and Gentile in the church, "For through him [Christ] we both have access in one Spirit to the Father" (Eph. 3:18 ESV). The movement, therefore, is *in* the Spirit, *through* the Son, *to* the Father. The Spirit himself ushers us through the Son into the very presence of the Father. This is true Christianity—Christianity in 3D, as we're calling it!

This reality points us further to the *priority* of the Father. Notice in Scripture that it is the Father himself who is most often referred to simply as God. It is the Father who sends the Son. It is the Father who through the Son supplies the Spirit. At the same time the Father's

---

10 Thomas A. Smail, *The Forgotten Father* (Grand Rapids: Eerdmans, 1980).

"fatherhood" is dependent upon the Son's "sonship" in the Spirit, so all three Persons are coequal and coeternal. The Son and the Spirit are in no way inferior to the Father. They are no less God than is the Father. "For the Father is known as the one God by the Son in the Holy Spirit."[11] So in that sense the ultimate Christian name for God is "Father, Son, and Holy Spirit."

> Christianity is really a Father movement...a movement *in* the Spirit, *through* the Son, *to* the Father.

Further, the Triune God acts both objectively and subjectively to bring about our redemption (Gal. 4:4–7): He sends his Son into *history* ("born of a woman, born under the law") and he sends the Spirit of his Son into our *hearts* ("who calls out, "*Abba*, Father"). Through this Spirit-inspired cry, "*Abba*, Father," we come to personal assurance that we are God's child. Through this witness of the Spirit (Rom 8:16) we come through Christ to a full *experience* of God as our Father.

Our whole concept of fatherhood comes from God and not vice versa. Indeed many of has have not been blessed with a healthy father-child relationship, if we had a father at home at all. The apostle Paul expressed it this way: "For this reason I kneel before the Father [*patera*], from whom every family [*patria*] in heaven and on earth derives its name" (Eph 3:14–15). In the swirl of confusing concepts of family and sexuality in Western cultures today, we need the Father's help more than ever to rediscover his original designs for us. Even the church flounders on these issues today. We have too often lost a firm grip on the Father's leadership and Jesus' lordship. But thanks be to God, the Spirit seems to be coming to our aid. "In the critical period in which we live, it appears that the Spirit is revealing anew the Fatherhood of God and the Lordship of Christ to a church that is

---

11 Wolfhart Pannenberg, *Systematic Theology*, trans. Geoffrey W. Bromiley, Vol. 1 (Grand Rapids: Eerdmans, 1991), 326.

increasingly falling under the spell of the mythologies and ideologies that mesmerize our culture."[12]

So God's revealed name of *Father* is crucial in our day. We commit an egregious, if not blasphemous, error in seeking to rename God. Our attempt to make Jesus merely *a* lord and not *the* Lord and the Father merely *a* father and not *the* Father introduces destructive forces against both the individual and society as a whole. Theologian Karl Barth spoke this truth forcefully:

> No human father, but God alone, is properly, truly and primarily Father. No human father is the creator of his child, the controller of its destiny, or is saviour from sin, guilt and death. No human father is by his word the source of it temporal and eternal life. In this proper, true and primary sense God— and He alone—is Father.[13]

And Donald Bloesch adds this helpful summary statement: "God as Father is an archetypal or foundational analogy, an analogy *sui generis*, since it throws light upon the human conception of father."[14]

I am eternally thankful that my heavenly Father blessed me with a godly earthly father. I have a vivid memory to this day of standing before the congregation of Second Baptist Church in Ft. Stockton, Texas, as a seven year old, having acknowledged Jesus Christ as my personal Lord and Savior. In good Southern Baptist fashion, people were filing by to shake my hand when my father leaned forward and hugged me. I broke into tears as I sensed the simultaneous hug of my heavenly Father. My parents exemplified both God's fatherly (protective and providing) and motherly (nurturing) characteristics. It was easier for me to believe in

---

12 Donald G. Bloesch, *The Battle for the Trinity* (Ann Arbor, Mich.: Vine Books/Servant Publications, 1985), 27.

13 Karl Barth, *Church Dogmatics: Index Volume with Aids for the Preacher*, ed. G. W. Bromiley & T. F. Torrance (Edinburgh: T. & T. Clark, 1997), 495; cited in Donald G. Bloesch, *Is the Bible Sexist?* Westchester, Ill.: Crossway Books, 1982), 77, fn 39.

14 Bloesch, *Is the Bible Sexist?* 77.

the goodness and generosity of my Father because of my parents, who both went to be with the Lord within four days of each other, having lived full and fruitful lives.

I am a father as well. Now I understand more than ever how much my parents sacrificed for me and how much my heavenly Father nourishes and cherishes me. I am extremely proud of all three of my children and would do anything to promote their health and happiness. In view of this reality, Jesus encourages us to pursue our heavenly Father and all that he has for us.

Ask, and it will be given you; search, and you will find; knock, and the door will be opened for you. For everyone who asks receives, and everyone who searches finds, and for everyone who knocks, the door will be opened. Is there anyone among you, who, if your child asks for bread will give a stone? Or if the child asks for a fish, will give a snake? If you then, who are evil, know how to give good gifts to your children, how much more will your Father in heaven give good things to those who ask him! (Matthew 7:7–11 NRSV).

How many of us actually enjoy this kind of a relationship with God? We can—and should!—through Jesus Christ our Lord. Jesus' address to God as *Abba*, "Daddy," models our own. It exemplifies a relationship of confidence, security, reverence, and obedience.[15]

This supernatural experience of knowing God as our Father is three-dimensional. "God decided to adopt us into his own family by bringing us to himself through Jesus Christ. This is what he wanted to do, and it gave him great pleasure. So we praise God for the glorious grace he has poured out on us who belong to his dear Son" (Eph. 1:5–6 NLT). "You received God's Spirit when he adopted you as his own children. Now we call him, 'Abba, Father.' For his Spirit joins with our spirit to affirm that

---

15   See Joachim Jeremias, *New Testament Theology* (New York: Charles Scribner's Sons, 1971), 67.

we are God's children" (Rom. 8:15–16 NLT). Our being God's daughters and sons is made possible by the Father, the Son, and the Holy Spirit. This is Christianity in 3D! A three-in-one/one-in-three God adopting us into his family! How do we conceptualize such a God?

The Eastern Church, which has much less trouble with mystery and paradox than we Westerners do, starts with God's threeness and then moves toward explaining his oneness. The Father is seen as the source of divinity and unity in the Godhead. He eternally "begets" the Son and "spirates" the Spirit. In the West, Christians have tended to begin with God's oneness and then move toward his threeness. The three Persons of the Godhead share equally in the one divine nature. Nowadays, there is a tendency among many toward a communal model, beginning with a Trinity of Persons in a profound unity of relationship. Millard Erickson summarizes it well: "The Trinity is a communion of three persons, three centers of consciousness, who exist and always have existed in union with one another and in dependence on one another."[16] This third approach emphasizes the divine essence of *love* which unites the Father, Son, and Spirit in a mutually dependent, mutually submissive, and mutually glorifying eternal fellowship—into which God invites us! Again, 3D Christianity!

Another insight that comes immediately to mind is that the Trinity is obviously the model for how we should relate to one another. So many things divide human beings—nation against nation, race against race, generation against generation, male against female. But our Triune God, in complete unity of love, has chosen to begin a whole new humanity through Jesus Christ. This new creation finds a unity in Christ that transcends all such divisions: "There is neither Jew nor Greek, neither slave nor free, nor is there male and female, for you are all one in Christ Jesus" (Gal. 3:28). We all stand equal before God. Christ has proven that each person is of infinite value. The church still struggles to embrace this vision, while we should be modeling it! Perhaps because we have

---

16   Millard J. Erickson, *God in Three Persons* (Grand Rapids: Baker Books, 1995), 331.

too often lost sight of the Triune nature of God we have also forgotten the call to unity.

Before he went to the cross, Jesus prayed for his disciples, and then he prayed for us:

> My prayer is not for them alone. I pray also for those who will believe in me through their message, that all of them may be one, Father, just as you are in me and I am in you. May they also be in us so that the world may believe that you have sent me. I have given them the glory that you gave me, that they may be one—I in them and you in me—so that they may be brought to complete unity. Then the world will know that you sent me and have loved them even as you have loved me (John 17:20–23).

Notice how this unity for which Jesus prayed is rooted in the Trinity. It pays great dividends to mediate on this passage and all the "unities" that are referred to here.

All of this is possible because of Jesus. Christians are Trinitarians because of Jesus. Most of his first followers came out of a strictly monotheistic Judaism. Yet early on they came to perceive that Jesus was more than a man, and they began to worship him. They factored Jesus into their monotheism, as it were. Then came the launching of the church on her end-time ministry at Pentecost. With the Spirit's executive leadership of this mission, the church moved even further in a Trinitarian direction. It took centuries to formulate a formal doctrine of the Trinity, but their *experience* of the Trinity was formative from the outset! But, again, all this happened because of Jesus. It's time to take a closer look at the Son.

CHAPTER TWO
SON

At a key turning-point in his ministry, Jesus took his disciples aside to a very unusual retreat center. Caesarea Philippi was a beautiful pagan religious center on the slopes of Mt. Hermon, far to the north of Jesus' normal ministry travel routes. Jesus' purpose for his disciples evidently was one of consolidation and preparation for his coming passion. Matthew's account of this event is the most detailed:

> When Jesus came to the region of Caesarea Philippi, he asked his disciples, "Who do people say the Son of Man is?"
>
> They replied, "Some say John the Baptist; others Elijah; and still others, Jeremiah or one of the prophets."
>
> "But what about you?" he asked. "Who do you say I am?"
>
> Simon Peter answered, "You are the Messiah, the Son of the living God."
>
> Jesus replied, "Blessed are you, Simon son of Jonah, for this was not revealed to you by flesh and blood, but by my Father in heaven" (Matt. 16:13–17).

One can sense the urgency of Jesus. He is concerned that his disciples truly discern his identity and purpose. And he congratulates Peter for the correct response to the question, informing this impetuous disciple that this understanding had come to Peter by revelation from "my Father in heaven." Peter confessed that Jesus was the Messiah of Jewish hopes. The kingly deliverer for which the Jews had longed for centuries was also the kingly "Son of the living God," said Peter.

Earlier, Jesus had made a similar connection between himself and the Father, saying, "No one knows the Son except the Father, and no one knows the Father except the Son and those to whom the Son chooses to reveal him" (Matt. 11:27; see also Luke 10:22). Scholars often refer to this unique passage as a veritable "Johannine bolt out of the blue" because John's gospel is replete with this "Father/Son" talk from the lips of our Lord, whereas it is rare in the first three gospels. Jesus as "the Son" became all-important to the church in her formative years. People were baptized "in the name of the Father and of the Son and of the Holy Spirit" (Matt. 28:19), as our Lord commanded. The later creeds such as the *Nicene Creed* (325) and the *Definition of Chalcedon* (451) would highlight this Christological title of Son. James D. G. Dunn has observed:

> These creedal formulations have stamped a clear and lasting impression on Christian thought of subsequent generations up to and including the present day. So much so that it is generally taken for granted, axiomatic, part of the basic definition of what Christianity is, that to confess Jesus as "the Son of God" is to confess his deity, and very easily assumed that to say "Jesus is the Son of God" means and always has meant that Jesus is the pre-existent, second person of the Trinity, who "for us men and our salvation became incarnate."[1]

In his own day, Jesus' Jewish opponents were particularly scandalized by the unique relationship Jesus claimed to have with God as his Father. For them, "calling God his own Father" was tantamount to "making himself equal with God" (John 5:18), which

---

1 James D. G. Dunn, *Christology in the Making* (Philadelphia: Westminster, 1980), 12-13.

in their view was blasphemy. Jesus in turn responded, in good law court fashion, that there were at least five witnesses to the veracity of his filial claims: (1) the Father himself (vv. 32, 37); (2) John the Baptist (vv. 33–35); (3) Jesus' own works that the Father had sent him to complete (v. 36); (4) the Scriptures (vv. 39–40); and (5) even Moses, whom Jesus said "wrote about me" (vv. 46–47). In effect, Jesus was saying, "Don't miss the forest for the trees! Isn't it obvious that the Father is in me and working through me? Look and listen! See the signs! Hear my teachings! Read the Scriptures! All these 'witnesses' make it obvious who I am."

Jesus said to the Jewish leaders who were rejecting him, "You search the Scriptures because you think they give you eternal life. But the Scriptures point to me! Yet you refuse to come to me to receive this life" (John 5:39–40 NLT). Jesus wasn't diminishing the importance of the Scriptures. In fact, he appealed explicitly to their authority for his entire message and ministry. But he was saying that if you miss their central message—which is Christ!—you've missed it all. "Jesus saw his mission as the fulfillment of the Old Testament Scriptures; not just of those which predicted a coming redeemer, but of the whole sweep of Old Testament ideas."[2]

John Stott summarized this insight well:

> Jesus is the focus of Scripture. The Bible is not a random
> collection of religious documents. As Jesus himself said,
> "The Scriptures . . . bear witness to me" (John 5:39 RSV). And
> Christian scholars have always recognized this. For example,
> Jerome, the great church father of the fourth and fifth centuries,
> wrote that "ignorance of the Scriptures is ignorance of Christ"

---

2 R. T. France, *Jesus and the Old Testament* (Vancouver, BC: Regent College Pub., 1998), 79-90; cited in Leonard Sweet and Frank Viola, *Jesus: A Theography* (Nashville: Thomas Nelson, 2012), xiv. Sweet's and Viola's treatment of the centrality of Christ is unsurpassed: See also their *Jesus Manifesto* (Nashville: Thomas Nelson, 2010).

... Luther similarly, in his *Lectures on Romans*, was clear that Christ is the key to Scripture.[3]

Christians see things in the Hebrew Scriptures which their Jewish friends too often miss precisely because Christians read these Scriptures with "Christological lenses," as Jesus himself taught us to do and as the Holy Spirit enables us to do.

Unfortunately, much of American Christianity has lost this focus. We've become quite sophisticated in our ecclesial enterprises, enamored with just about everything but Jesus. William Willimon has a prophetic word for us:

> Here we are in the North American church—conservative or liberal, evangelical or mainline, Protestant or Catholic, emergent or otherwise—cranking along just fine, thank you. So we're busy downsizing, becoming culturally relevant, reaching out, drawing in, making disciples, managing the machinery, utilizing biblical principles, celebrating recovery, user-friendly, techno savvy, finding the purposeful life, practicing peace with justice, utilizing spiritual disciplines, growing in self-esteem, reinventing ourselves as effective ecclesiastical entrepreneurs, and, in general, feeling ever so much better about our achievements.
>
> Notice anything missing in this pretty picture? *Jesus Christ!*[4]

And now we have begun to decline ... almost to the place of alarm! So what do we do? Baptists consider name changes and redouble their evangelistic efforts. Charismatics jump a little higher and shout a

---

3 John Stott, *The Incomparable Christ* (Downers Grove, Ill.: InterVarsity, 2001), 15; cited in Sweet and Viola, *Jesus: A Theography*, 326.

4 From Willimon's foreword to: Michael Horton, *Christless Christianity* (Grand Rapids: Baker, 2008), 9.

little louder. Mainline groups try marketing in the media. But still we decline. We're closing more churches than we're planting. Our cultural influence is waning. Have we forsaken the love we used to have for Christ and one another (Rev. 2:4)? Has Jesus gotten lost in the shuffle of frantic religious activity? Can we call ourselves actual *followers* of Christ anymore? In effect, we've settled for "two-dimensional" Christianity, focusing more on our religious selves than on our risen Savior. But Christianity in 3D nudges us in the direction of a sincere devotion to the person of Christ himself and an adventurous, supernatural lifestyle of actually knowing and following him.

> We've settled for "two-dimensional" Christianity, focusing more on our religious selves than on our risen Savior.

The Centrality of Christ

In 3D Christianity the Son is the focus. Everything is about him. He is the meaning of the universe and of our lives. He is *the* love of our life. And this love enhances all of our other loving relationships. When we read our Bibles, we see him *everywhere*! We note that everything in the Old Testament leads up to him and everything in the New Testament branches out from him. He is the center of the Bible. He is the center of history. He is the meaning of both time and eternity. When our eyes pop open each morning, we turn to him to find out what's on the agenda today. It's all about him—not us!

I teach systematic theology in a seminary. And one of the most important things I try to impress upon my students is how Jesus is the center of it all. My mentor when I was in seminary was Dale Moody, who defined theology as follows: "A Christian theology is an effort to think coherently about the basic beliefs that create a community of faith around the person of Jesus Christ."[5] Every central Christian doctrine has Christ at its center. Consider the doctrines of revelation, God, creation, humanity, sin, Christology (the person and work of Christ), pneumatology (the person and work of the Holy Spirit), soteriology (the doctrines of salvation), ecclesiology (the church), and eschatology (the end times).

1. **Revelation:** The greatest revelation of God is Jesus Christ, who is God Incarnate.
2. **God:** To see Jesus truly is to see the Father (in all his attributes) and to discern Jesus' unique triune union with the Father (John 14:9–11).
3. **Creation:** Creation is through Christ and for Christ, who both sustains and redeems his creation.
4. **Humanity:** Jesus is the supreme example of humanity— the only complete human being, reflecting perfectly the divine image.
5. **Sin:** The reason Jesus came was to be the sin bearer and the victor over sin, death, and the devil.
6. **Christology:** It is through the person and work of Christ that we are saved.
7. **Pneumatology:** The Holy Spirit—referred to variously in the New Testament as the Spirit of Christ, the Spirit of Jesus, the Spirit of God's Son—applies Christ's saving work in our lives.
8. **Soteriology:** God saves us in and through Christ.
9. **Ecclesiology:** The church is the Body of Christ and the Bride of Christ.
10. **Eschatology:** Jesus is coming again!

Further, as we study the history of Christian thought, we discover that almost all of the doctrinal aberrations, the heresies that distort or deny the true faith, in some way relate to Jesus.

---

5   Dale Moody, *The Word of Truth* (Grand Rapids: Eerdmans, 1981), 1.

At the Council of Chalcedon in 451, the church rightly concluded that there are four foundational truths concerning Christ: (1) He is God; (2) he is human; (3) he is one person; and (4) he has two natures, divine and human. Here's how the ancient heresies distorted these biblical truths, and these are the same heresies we deal with today, only with different labels and terminology.

First, Jesus is God: Some simply denied this truth (Ebionism), while others (Arianism) distorted it by saying that Jesus was a creature of God through whom God created and redeemed humanity (in other words, Jesus was not fully God).

Second, Jesus is human: Some rejected this truth altogether (Docetism), while others distorted it by arguing that Jesus was not fully human (Apollinarianism). Jesus' rational soul or mind was displaced by the pre-existent Logos (Son).

Third, Jesus is one person: Some (Nestorianism) compromised the unity of the person of Christ, arguing that the pre-existent Son of God indwelled the independently existing Jesus of Nazareth. In other words, Jesus was actually the conjoining of two distinct persons, a monster rather than the God-Man.

Fourth, Jesus has two natures, divine and human: Some argued that Jesus had one blended nature (Eutychianism), usually understood as the swallowing up of the human nature by the divine nature.[6] It is obvious that we are wrestling with the same distortions in our own day. The reason they must be refuted and rejected is the very gospel itself is at stake.

John gave his beautiful portrayal of Jesus with a singular purpose in mind: "Jesus performed many other signs in the presence of his disciples, which are not recorded in this book. But these are written that you may believe that Jesus is the Messiah, the Son of God, and that by believing you may have life in his name" (John 20:30–32). God gave us his Son

---

6   See Millard J. Erickson's excellent chart on these six heresies in *Introducing Christian Doctrine*, 2d ed. (Grand Rapids: Baker Academic, 2001), 239.

that we may have eternal life (John 3:16). How so? The gospel tells us how. Paul put it down in bullet points (1 Cor. 15:3–8):

- Christ died for our sins according to the Scriptures.
- He was buried.
- He was raised on the third day according to the Scriptures.
- He appeared to many (Peter, the Twelve, a gathering of more than five hundred, James, and Paul himself).

Now we come to the core of 3D Christianity—the cross of Christ.

The Meaning of the Cross

The apostle Paul reminded the Corinthian believers that the message of "Christ crucified" was scandalous to sign-seeking Jews and moronic to wisdom-seeking Gentiles (1 Cor. 1:22–23). But for those of us who by grace have believed the gospel that was preached to us, Christ is the wisdom of God and the power of God (v. 24). Christ himself is our wisdom from God, that is, our righteousness, our holiness, and our freedom (v. 30). And the gospel "is the power of God that brings salvation to everyone who believes: first to the Jew, then to the Gentile" (Rom. 1:16). To the world, the message of the cross is profoundly puzzling. Are we to believe that the death of a first-century Jewish man, Jesus of Nazareth, hanging on a Roman cross outside the city wall of Jerusalem, was God's way of saving humanity? Absolutely! We glory in the cross of the risen Savior who "was delivered over to death for our sins and raised to life for our justification" (Rom. 4:25). Let me give you five words to summarize the meaning of the cross: love, judgment, deliverance, sacrifice, and substitution.

First, love: The cross of Christ is the greatest revelation of the love of God for sinful humanity. "For God so loved the world that he gave his one and only Son, that whoever believes in him shall not perish but have eternal life" (John 3:16). Martin Luther, the great Reformer, taught that you come to saving faith by God's grace when you realize that Jesus Christ died for you personally. Jesus himself said, "Greater love has no one than this: to lay down one's life for one's friends" (John15:13). Paul summarized this insight into God's saving love with these words:

> You see, at just the right time, when we were still powerless, Christ died for the ungodly. Very rarely will anyone die for a righteous person, though for a good person someone might possibly dare to die. But God demonstrates his own love for us in this: While we were still sinners, Christ died for us (Rom. 5:6–8).

It was "while we were God's enemies" that "we were reconciled to him through the death of his Son" (v. 10). "God was reconciling the world to himself in Christ, not counting people's sins against them" (2 Cor. 5:19). That was love!

"This is love: not that we loved God, but that he loved us and sent his Son as an atoning sacrifice for our sins" (1 John 4:10). "God made him [Christ] who had no sin to be sin for us, so that in him we might become the righteousness of God" (2 Cor. 5:21). The apostle Peter reminds us that "Christ suffered for you" (1 Peter 2: 21). We too often forget this. Mel Gibson did us all a favor with his film depicting the suffering involved in the passion of the Christ. Christ suffered physically, mentally, emotionally, and spiritually for us. He died the awful death that we all deserve to die. He offers us a new covenant in his blood (1 Cor. 11:25), and he is the mediator of a better covenant with better promises (Heb. 8:6). Those of us who believe "are now justified by his grace as a gift, through the redemption that is in Christ Jesus, whom God put forward as a sacrifice of atonement by his blood, effective through faith" (Rom. 3:24–25 NRSV).

Jesus was God's Suffering Servant, about whom Isaiah wrote some seven centuries before Christ. Isaiah's words read like a newspaper account of the crucifixion (Isa. 52:13–53:12 NLT):

The Lord's Suffering Servant

¹³ See, my servant will prosper;
  he will be highly exalted.
¹⁴ But many were amazed when they saw him.
  His face was so disfigured he seemed hardly human,
and from his appearance, one would scarcely know he
  was a man.
¹⁵ And he will startle many nations.
  Kings will stand speechless in his presence.
For they will see what they had not been told;
  they will understand what they had not heard about.

53 Who has believed our message?
  To whom has the LORD revealed his powerful arm?
² My servant grew up in the LORD's presence like a tender
  green shoot, like a root in dry ground.
There was nothing beautiful or majestic about his
  appearance, nothing to attract us to him.
³ He was despised and rejected—a man of sorrows,
  acquainted with deepest grief.
We turned our backs on him and looked the other way.
  He was despised, and we did not care.

⁴ Yet it was our weaknesses he carried;
  it was our sorrows that weighed him down.

And we thought his troubles were a punishment from
  God, a punishment for his own sins!
5 But he was pierced for our rebellion,
  crushed for our sins.
He was beaten so we could be whole.
  He was whipped so we could be healed.
6 All of us, like sheep, have strayed away.
  We have left God's paths to follow our own.
Yet the LORD laid on him
  the sins of us all.

7 He was oppressed and treated harshly,
  yet he never said a word.
He was led like a lamb to the slaughter.
  And as a sheep is silent before the shearers,
  he did not open his mouth.
8 Unjustly condemned,
  he was led away.
No one cared that he died without descendants,
  that his life was cut short in midstream.
But he was struck down
  for the rebellion of my people.
9 He had done no wrong
  and had never deceived anyone.
But he was buried like a criminal;
  he was put in a rich man's grave.

10 But it was the LORD's good plan to crush him
  and cause him grief.
Yet when his life is made an offering for sin,
  he will have many descendants.

He will enjoy a long life,
  and the LORD's good plan will prosper in his hands.
[11] When he sees all that is accomplished by his anguish,
  he will be satisfied.
And because of his experience,
  my righteous servant will make it possible
for many to be counted righteous,
  for he will bear all their sins.
[12] I will give him the honors of a victorious soldier,
  because he exposed himself to death.
He was counted among the rebels.
  He bore the sins of many and interceded for rebels.

Jesus endured the judgment we justly deserved, which brings us to our second word summarizing the meaning of the cross: judgment.

The cross is God's judgment on our sin. Many of us are familiar with the wonderful announcement of Romans chapter 8, verse 1, that "there is now no condemnation for those who are in Christ Jesus." What we may not be as fully aware of is the theme of judgment in this passage. Those of us in Christ face no condemnation, no judgment, no punishment. Hallelujah! But how is this possible? The law of Moses was powerless to free us from "the law of sin and death." So God sets another law in place, "the law of the Spirit of life," which "in Christ Jesus" sets us free from the law of sin and death. What Moses' law could not do "God did by sending his own Son in the likeness of sinful flesh to be a sin offering [atonement]. And so he condemned [the verb form of the noun in verse 1] sin in the flesh" (v. 3) to enable holy living! God judged our sin at Calvary! (We will look more closely at this passage later when we consider the work of the Holy Spirit in empowering holy living.) Our sin has already been judged—no condemnation!

Jesus himself also taught that his cross was God's judgment on our sin. The two verses before the famous sixteenth verse of John chapter 3 explain this: "And just as Moses lifted up the serpent in the wilderness, so must the Son of Man be lifted up, that whoever believes in him may have eternal life" (John 3:14–15 NRSV). The story to which Jesus referred is found in Numbers 21:4–9. God's people were murmuring against God and his servant Moses in the wilderness, and God sent judgment in the form of venomous snakes, bringing a painful death to those who were bitten. Moses interceded in prayer, and God instructed him to make a bronze replica of the snake and put it on a pole. Whoever was bitten could simply look at the snake and live. The snake then became symbolic of both God's judgment on their sin as well as his deliverance from that judgment. So it is at the cross. On the cross of Christ, God judged the sins of humanity. And through that same cross he offers us forgiveness.

One other concept is closely related to this theme of judgment and that is the wrath of God. The cross was the means of God's turning away his wrath against our sins. Both the apostles Paul and John make reference to this important significance of Christ's atonement. Paul announces that "God presented Christ as a sacrifice of atonement, through the shedding of his blood—to be received by faith" (Rom. 3:25). The phrase "sacrifice of atonement" translates the Greek term *hilasterion*. In the Day of Atonement chapter of Leviticus, chapter 16, the Septuagint (the Greek translation of the Hebrew Scriptures) uses this term to translate the Hebrew for the mercy-seat, the cover of the arch of the covenant, the place of propitiation, where the blood of the sin offering was sprinkled (Lev. 16:15–16). Propitiation signifies the averting of wrath. In other words, on the cross, God in Christ absorbed back into himself all the wrath and judgment upon our sins that we deserved.

The apostle John makes reference to this same reality in 1 John. "This is love: not that we loved God, but that he loved us and sent his Son as an atoning sacrifice for our sins" (1 John 4:10). The phrase "atoning sacrifice" translates the Greek *hilasmos*, meaning sin offering, propitiation, or expiation. Expiation would refer to the removal of the defilement of our sins. Earlier, John had pointed to the Son as our "advocate with the Father—Jesus Christ the Righteous One. He is the atoning sacrifice [*hilasmos*] for our sins, and not only for ours but also for the sins of the whole world" (1 John 2:1–2). Jesus, the Son of God, made all of this possible!

Jesus was on a rescue mission: "For the Son of Man came to seek and to save the lost" (Luke 19:10). This brings us to our fourth word, deliverance. Jesus Christ came to deliver us from sin, the condemnation of the law, death, and the devil. Sin in Scripture is much more than the things we say, do, and think wrong. It is a state of being. It is a power that holds us in sway. And only the death of Christ can remedy the situation. First, we need deliverance from sin. We have already touched on this and much more will need to be said later. But at this juncture, the key concept we need to grasp is our identification with Christ in his death on our behalf.

> Jesus Christ came to deliver us from sin, the condemnation of the law, death, and the devil.

Paul succinctly states this liberating truth in one sentence: "We know that our old self was crucified with him so that the body of sin might be destroyed, and we might no longer be enslaved to sin" (Rom. 6:6 NRSV). As we will study later, the Holy Spirit applies the death of Jesus in our lives to liberate us from the insidious influence of sin.

We have also been liberated by Jesus' atoning death from the condemnation of the law. The law serves as a mirror to point up God's righteous standards and our shortcomings, but it is powerless to free us from this plight of spiritual bondage. The apostle Paul described for the Colossian believers how God has forgiven us and made us alive in Christ and how he delivers us from the condemnation of the law as well as the devil and his minions, which he leads away as a conquered army: "God wiped out the charges that were against us for disobeying the Law of Moses. He took them away and nailed them to the cross. There Christ defeated all powers and forces. He let the whole world see them being led away as prisoners when he celebrated his victory" (Col. 2:14–15 CEV). At the same time, Christ defeated once and for all the death that reigns over fallen humanity.

"We are people of flesh and blood. That is why Jesus became one of us. He died to destroy the devil, who had power over death. But he also died to rescue all of us who live each day in fear of dying" (Heb. 2:14–15 CEV). The last enemy to be conquered is death. Death is total in every generation. Yet for the believer it is different. The New Testament uses the descriptive phrase of "falling asleep in Jesus." Jesus said, "Everyone who lives in me and believes in me will never ever die" (John 11:26 NLT). So we actually have eternal life now and death is only a transition to glory! That's good news! Christ is risen. That old nemesis death has been defeated. "Death has been swallowed up in victory" (1 Cor. 15:54). Two more words describe what our Lord did for us on the cross: sacrifice and substitution.

The idea of an atoning *sacrifice* seems foreign to most of us in the twenty-first century. It's the reason we often tend to skip over Leviticus in our daily Bible readings. The idea of priests offering blood sacrifices is foreign and quite frankly offensive to us at times. Perhaps one of the reasons this is so stems from our neglect of the Old Testament and our failure to see its fulfillment in the New Testament. The writer of Hebrews has done our homework for us! He shows how Jesus in his atoning death on our behalf was both our high priest and the sacrifice itself, dealing with our sin problem once and for all. "But Christ offered himself as a sacrifice that is good forever. Now he is sitting at God's right side, and he will stay there until his enemies are put under his power. By his one sacrifice he has forever set free from sin the people he brings to God" (Heb. 10:12–14 CEV). Christ is our "advocate with the Father" (1 John 2:2).

"Because Jesus lives forever, he has a permanent priesthood. Therefore he is able to save completely those who come to God through him, because he always lives to intercede for them" (Heb. 7:24–25 CEV). Jesus was the sin bearer, and in that sense he was also our *substitute*.

Some scholars resist this idea of substitution, but the logic of the atonement demands it. Isaiah said of Christ: "The LORD has laid on him the iniquity of us all" (Isa. 53:6 NRSV). The apostle Peter wrote: "He himself bore our sins in his body on the cross" (1 Peter 2:24 NRSV). John the Baptist introduced our Lord dramatically: "Behold, the Lamb of God who takes away the sin of the world!" (John 1:29 NASB). Christ as our *substitute* endures the just penalty of our sin, thus providing acquittal and forgiveness.

Our response to the passion of the Christ should be at least fivefold:
- Repentance: acknowledging and turning away from our sins
- Faith: trusting in Christ's atoning death *alone*
- Adoration: praising and thanking Christ continually
- Service: sharing Christ's love with others
- Sacrifice: taking up our cross daily

Every person needs to encounter Jesus. Everyone needs a testimony. We need to be able to bear witness to the reality of Jesus Christ residing in our lives. God's gift of eternal life is all wrapped up in Jesus. The apostle John summarizes it well: "And this is the testimony: God has given us eternal life, and this life is in his Son. Whoever has the Son has life; whoever does not have the Son of God does not have life. I write these things to you who believe in the name of the Son of God so that you may know that you have eternal life" (1 John 5:11–13). The following is my own personal testimony to having the Son of God and knowing that I have eternal life.

My Testimony

I grew up on the flat, hot, dry, barren plains of West Texas. As far as the eye could see there were oil wells, jack rabbits, tumbleweeds, mesquite trees (really, bushes no taller than a person's head), and sometimes rattlesnakes. My dad worked for Texaco oil company. Until I was in the third grade, we lived in what were known as oil camps—a small collection of white frame houses outside of town near the oil leases. Oil was what put most of the towns in this region on the map. Odessa, which I always considered my hometown until the Lord called my parents home, grew to a population of almost 100,000, because of the oil boom. Sixteen miles away another town of comparable size, Midland, stood as a sort of capital for the region. The oil bosses lived in nice homes in Midland and worked out of clean, shiny office buildings. The oil field workers lived in Odessa in more modest dwellings with their dingy offices out among the oil leases themselves.

We lived and died by oil. Odessa went from being the town with the lowest unemployment rate in the country to being the one with the highest murder rate per capita. Boom to bust—and back again. Only the last bust seemed to be a permanent one. In recent years, however, the region has seemed to be making a comeback.

There were two main religions where I came from. First was Christianity, primarily of the Southern Baptist or Church of Christ varieties. The Methodists and few others held their own as well. The other religion was football. Public worship for this faith took place every Friday night when hundreds and even thousands would gather under the lights to watch their boys butt heads on the field. Years later, a Pulitzer Prize-winning author would even write a book about my high school football team. He chose a great title: *Friday Night Lights*. But he also made a lot of people mad because they came out looking like bigoted, red-neck, fanatical ignoramuses.

I became a Christian when I was seven years old. We were living at that time in an oil camp outside of Fort Stockton, Texas. For about a year I would squirm in the pew every Sunday morning when the "invitation" was being given to "accept Christ." I sensed the moving of the Holy Spiri, convicting me of sin. I understood very little of the Sunday sermons I heard, but one enormous truth did get across: If I had been the only person in this world, Jesus would have died for me. Later in my seminary studies I would learn that this was a profound theological insight. The great Reformer, Martin Luther, discovered in his quest for personal assurance of faith—that is, knowing that you have eternal life, as we read in 1 John—that true saving faith involved trusting in Christ alone for salvation in the conviction that Jesus had died not just for mankind in general but for you in particular.

I will never forget the day I encountered Jesus as long as I live. I was gripping the back of the pew in front of me with white knuckles during the "invitation" time, wanting desperately to walk to the front, take the pastor's hand, and tell him I wanted Jesus in my life. My mom looked at me and asked if I was ill. I turned to her and simply said, "Oh, Mama, I want to become a Christian." But the invitation ended at that moment, and I thought, as a seven year old, that I would have to wait until next Sunday! My parents took me to the pastor after the service had ended and we went to his study for further counsel.

What happened to me next changed my life. Sitting there in a metal folding chair in the pastor's study, I prayed a simple prayer asking the Lord to forgive me and to come into my life. Then something supernatural happened which I have never been able to explain. A light came into me. I felt as if I were face to face with Jesus. The weight of sin lifted off me. Thinking in football terms, I felt as if shoulder pads came off me. When I went to my elementary school the next day, I couldn't understand why everything looked the same because I was completely different. Later I would learn that the apostle Paul had described this transformation well: "Therefore, if anyone is in Christ, the new creation has come: The old is gone, the new is here!" (2 Cor. 5:17). I now had the Son of God. I now had eternal life.

As often happens with childhood conversions, when I entered adolescence I came to own the faith in a new way. I was so impressed with the testimonies of my aunt Lou and uncle Wilbur. Aunt Lou was my mom's twin sister—Sara Sue and Ella Lue, Sue and Lue—and Wilbur was the son of a Pentecostal minister. I envied their vibrant joy and intimacy with Jesus. And their testimony was that the Holy Spirit made this all possible. So I began to pursue the Holy Spirit. The summer after I graduated from high school, in a youth seminar at Oral Roberts University, I had another dramatic encounter with Jesus.

I found myself in a prayer room begging Jesus to fill me with his Holy Spirit. Pat Robertson, a Southern Baptist senator's son from Virginia, who was just getting his Christian Broadcasting Network started, came into the prayer room and gave me wise counsel. He said, "Larry, you don't have to beg the Lord to fill you with his Holy Spirit. He has commanded you to be filled with his Spirit" (Eph. 5:18). He told me that I should ask and receive by faith, just as when I asked for forgiveness as a child. And what happened next would be another turning point in my life. Again, I was face to face with Jesus, the light of his presence engulfing me. I began to pray in a language I had never learned. But I was not noticing the new tongues of prayer and praise. I was noticing Jesus. I felt I was in the throne room of the Father. I was caught up for hours worshiping the Lord in a liberty I had never experienced before.

That encounter launched me into ministry. I was sharing my faith with greater effectiveness. My own pastor back in Odessa even had me preach on Sunday morning in our big Southern Baptist church. I spoke at youth retreats and other events. My parents, my pastor, my best friend, and his pastor all knew something dramatic had happened in my life, even though they didn't understand certain aspects of my testimony, such as speaking in tongues! I didn't either, for that matter! But I knew Jesus was more real to me than ever. His Word, the Bible, was more alive to me. And my witness to Christ was definitely more effective.

Later I would learn that my experience was commonplace in New Testament times. The Book of Acts is filled with similar stories. I would also discover that there are millions of Christians today with a similar testimony. In fact, at present there are some six hundred million of them—Christians variously labeled as Pentecostals or charismatics. And that brings us to our next topic of exploration: the person and work of the Holy Spirit.

CHAPTER THREE
HOLY SPIRIT

Thanks to the apostle John, we have been given glimpses into the inner sanctum of the Triune Godhead. John, more than any other Bible writer, delineates the Father, Son, and Holy Spirit and demonstrates their interrelatedness. And through his unique gospel tradition, we are permitted to hear from Jesus himself about the Father and the Spirit and the inner relations among the three. Only because of John do we have Jesus' in-depth teaching on the Holy Spirit. It is found in what is often called the Upper Room Discourse, in John, chapters 13–17.

What we immediately apprehend in these teachings of Jesus is the personhood of the Spirit. The Holy Spirit is too often referred to as "it" in Christian conversation. This is understandable for several reasons. First, he is the only Person of the Godhead without a name. He derives his names from the Father and the Son. He is the "Go-Between God," as John V. Taylor describes him in Taylor's classic volume by that name.[1] The Spirit is primarily understood in relational terms as the bond between the Father and Son and between God and us. Second, the metaphors for the Spirit in the Scriptures that depict his powerful impact—metaphors such as wind, fire, and water—can easily be taken in impersonal terms and we thus might mistakenly miss that he is a divine *Person*. But Jesus' teachings on the Spirit in the Upper Room explode this erroneous conclusion.

---

1   John V. Taylor, *The Go-Between God: The Holy Spirit and the Christian Mission* (London: SCM, 1972).

So our first task will be to give careful consideration to our Lord's teachings on this matter. Then we will broaden our focus to complete a broad stroke portrayal of the Holy Spirit from the Scriptures. Jesus uses an unusual term in these teachings to refer to the Holy Spirit: *Parakletos*. This Greek word refers to someone who serves as an advocate in a law court, providing defense and counsel. The term itself—*para*, "alongside" and *kletos*, "called"—indicates this dynamic. Thus, the Holy Spirit is our advocate, called alongside us to counsel and defend us. Immediately we see how *relational* the Spirit is. In the Bible we find this term *parakletos* only in the writings of John. In 1 John it is used of Jesus himself, who is described as our "advocate with the Father." And in chapters 14 through 16 of John's gospel Jesus uses it in reference to the Spirit. Scholars have delineated five "Paraclete Sayings" in these chapters. Each saying, or teaching, has a distinctive emphasis. The Holy Spirit is variously depicted as helper, teacher, witness, judge, and guide. And the sayings are couched in a profoundly Trinitarian setting. It is truly an edifying experience to give a careful hearing to each one! These teachings could be displayed as follows:

1. **HELPER:** John 14:15–24—Through the Father's giving us the Spirit the Trinity takes up residence within us.
2. **TEACHER:** John 14:25–26—The Father will send us the Spirit to continue Jesus' teaching ministry among us.
3. **WITNESS:** John 15:26–27—Jesus sends the Spirit from the Father to empower our witness.
4. **JUDGE:** John 16:4–11—Jesus leaves the earth bodily in order to send the Spirit, who will convict the world of sin.
5. **GUIDE:** John 16:12–15—The Holy Spirit guides us into all truth, the things of Jesus and the Father.

Helper

First, the Holy Spirit is our *helper*. It is the night before his crucifixion and Jesus knows everything will be different for his disciples from now on. He wants to comfort them, encourage them, and instruct them about a new and more intimate relationship that they will have with him in the near future—despite the trauma of Calvary they will soon witness. He talks about preparing a place for them and returning and taking them to be with him (John 14:1–4). He elaborates more on his union with the Father and on his being the way to the Father (vv. 5–14). And then he promises them the Holy Spirit.

"If you love me, keep my commands. And I will ask the Father, and he will give you another advocate to help you and be with you forever—the Spirit of truth" (vv.15–17). There are two key words for another in Greek: *allos*, another of the same kind; and *heteros*, another of a different kind. Jesus uses the former here. The Holy Spirit is "another of the same kind," Jesus' *alter ego*, as it were![2] Jesus was the disciples' Paraclete on earth, while with them bodily. Later he would serve in the same capacity with the Father in heaven after his resurrection and ascension (1 John 2:1). But soon they would be receiving the Holy Spirit, another advocate who would be with them forever.

Then Jesus adds: "The world cannot accept him, because it neither sees him nor knows him" (v. 17). The word "accept" is intriguing. Any seminarian who has had a beginning Greek class can tell you that the aorist infinitive here, *labein*, can be translated as either "receive" (accept) or "take." These are two widely differing concepts in our

---

2   I owe this concept to two persons: (1) Oral Roberts, who I often heard referring to the Holy Spirit as "more of Jesus" and "Jesus' *alter ego*"; and (2) the renowned Bible scholar, the late F. F. Bruce: *The Gospel of John* (Grand Rapids: Eerdmans, 1983), 302.

language, and only the context can help us determine which is the better translation. The world was going to take the *visible* Paraclete, Jesus, and torture and crucify him. But they would not be able to take the *invisible* Paraclete, the Holy Spirit, and do the same to him![3] And notice that Jesus refers here to "the world" (*kosmos*), referring to fallen humanity, rebelling against God and his rightful authority. Thus, it is also true that "accept" could be the best translation, since, as Jesus says, "it neither sees him [the Spirit] nor knows him" (v. 17). Spiritual things are moronic to fallen humanity (1 Cor. 2:14), Paul would remind us. Thus, both translations are possible—and they are not mutually exclusive!

"But you know him," Jesus quickly adds, "for he lives with you and will be in you" (John 14:17). The Holy Spirit is *with* them now—in Jesus—and will soon be *in* them. On Easter Sunday night Jesus appeared to them, breathed on them, and said, "Receive [same verb as in John 14:17!] the Holy Spirit" (John 20:22). Notice Jesus told them that they already knew the Holy Spirit: They knew him in Jesus, just as they knew the Father in Jesus. Philip had said, "Lord, show us the Father and that will be enough for us" (John 14:8). And Jesus had replied, "Don't you know me, Philip, even after I have been among you such a long time. Anyone who has seen me has seen the Father" (v. 9). "Don't you believe that I am in the Father, and that the Father is in me," Jesus asked further (v. 10). This is a profound Trinitarian reality. Jesus promised them that they would see him again after his death and resurrection: "On that day you will realize that I am in my Father, and you are in me, and I am in you" (v. 20). Jesus also said that included with this coming of the Paraclete would be Jesus and the Father: "Anyone who loves me will obey my teaching. My father will love them, and we will come to them and make our home with them" (v. 23). *Therefore, Jesus was teaching that through the*

3   Dale Moody, *Spirit of the Living God* (Philadelphia: Westminster, 1968), 165-66.

indwelling of the Holy Spirit, we become a home for the Trinity, the Father, the Son, and the Holy Spirit! That's Christianity in 3D! But how many of us who believe fully appreciate—and appropriate!—this marvelous transforming reality?

We need help. And Jesus has provided the Helper, the Holy Spirit. Through the Spirit's presence in our lives we also have both the Father and the Son indwelling us. That obviously means that we are more than equal to the tasks and tragedies life confronts us with, and that this Christian life is really all about God and not about us. Our experience of God was always meant to be Trinitarian. Theologian Fred Sanders has written profoundly about this in his book *The Deep Things of God: How the Trinity Changes Everything.*[4] Sanders has specialized in the doctrine of the Trinity in his scholarly pursuits and has an equal passion for helping folks enjoy the practical impact of knowing God as triune. Early on in his book, he introduces a person into the discussion that no one would have anticipated.

Sanders tells the story of Nicky Cruz, the violent street gang leader who was dramatically converted to Christ through the witness of David Wilkerson in 1953. In 1976 Cruz published a book on the Trinity entitled *The Magnificent Three.*[5] Sanders writes: "As a theologian whose speciality is Trinitarian theology, I have several hundred books about the Trinity on my shelves, but only one of them includes a knife fight: the one by Nicky Cruz."[6] Cruz had a life-reorienting encounter with Jesus and became a powerful evangelist. But it was years later before he came to appreciate the triune nature of God. Here is how he describes his discovery:

---

4   (Wheaton, Ill.: Crossway, 2010).
5   Nicky Cruz with Charles Paul Conn (Old Tappan, NJ: Revell, 1976).
6   Sanders, *The Deep Things of God*, 29.

Something has happened in me over those years of ministry that I would never have predicted. Something has emerged in my walk with God that has become the most important element of my discipleship. It has become the thing that sustains me, that feeds me, that keeps me steady when I am shaky. *I have come to see God, to know Him, to relate to Him as Three-in-One, God as Trinity, God as Father, Saviour, and Holy Spirit.*[7]

Cruz comments that he had always believed in the doctrine of the Trinity, but that now "it has become a truth of everyday life." He had learned to develop a relationship with each person of the Godhead and to derive strength from each of them. "He [God] has taught me to feed off the Trinity for my daily sustenance, rather than just having some vague feeling that the Trinity is somehow true."[8]

> We are comforted, guided, and taught by the Holy Spirit and empowered in our worship and witness.

This was precisely the insight Jesus was imparting in his Paraclete Sayings! In 3D Christianity, we have a separate relationship with each Person of the Trinity. We derive strength, stability, comfort, and discipline from the Father. We follow Jesus daily as he fishes for people—saving, healing, and transforming them. (And Jesus lets us in on the action!) And we are comforted, guided, and taught by the Holy Spirit and empowered in our worship and witness. The fact is, we need the triune God's help daily in every endeavor of life. For example, Jesus *taught* his disciples daily. And that teaching ministry continues today in our own lives through the Holy Spirit—which brings us to our next Paraclete Saying.

---

7   Cruz, *The Magnificent Three*, 16–17 (italics Cruz's).
8   Cruz, *The Magnificent Three*, 17.

Teacher

Teaching loomed large in the ministry of Jesus and in the life of the early church. And later we will give fuller attention to this important subject. In this second Paraclete saying Jesus highlights the teaching ministry of the Holy Spirit. It is interesting to note that this is the only time in the entire discourse that Jesus actually uses the phrase "Holy Spirit": "All this I have spoken while still with you. But the Advocate, the Holy Spirit, whom the Father will send in my name will teach you all things and will remind you of everything I have said to you" (John 14:25–26). Again, the Trinitarian pattern is evident: The Advocate, the Holy Spirit is sent by the Father in Jesus' name. Just as Jesus was sent by the Father (in the Father's *name*, John 5:43), so the Holy Spirit is sent by the Father *in Jesus' name*, that is, as representing Jesus.

The Spirit's ministry is centered on Jesus. He has a "reminding" ministry. "The Paraclete interprets the things said and done by Jesus."[9] For example, after Jesus cleared the temple, the Jews asked, "What sign can you show us to prove your authority to do all this?" Jesus responded with "Destroy this temple, and I will raise it again in three days," referring to his crucifixion and bodily resurrection. "After he was raised from the dead, his disciples recalled what he had said. Then they believed the scripture and the words that Jesus had spoken" (John 2:18–22). The Spirit continues this ministry to this day. "The church's memory of Jesus and his word is the particular work of the Holy Spirit."[10] Ultimately, the Holy Spirit gave us a book for this purpose—the Bible!

Too often charismatics lust after some new information, some new revelation from the Holy Spirit. In fact, they are often more excited by these "revelations" than the Scriptures themselves. They spend very little time prayerfully reading and studying the Bible. They will even record

---

9 Moody, *Spirit of the Living God*, 168.
10 George T. Montague, *The Holy Spirit: Growth of a Biblical Tradition* (New York: Paulist Press, 1976), 352.

prophecies and treat them like scriptures. And they are sitting ducks for all kinds of distortions and deceptions. *The Holy Spirit would have us centered on Jesus and on studying and obeying his teachings.* That is the essence of the teaching ministry of the Holy Spirit. He wants to enable us to make disciples, in part, by "teaching them to obey everything I have commanded you," as Jesus said in the Great Commission. In summary: "The ministry of the Paraclete is to be one of representation and remembrance."[11]

I have a vivid memory of my early seminary days. I was talking with a wise Southern Baptist pastor about my beginning the seminary pilgrimage. I expressed concern about what I would face in the classroom, since the seminary at that time had a liberal reputation. The pastor made an off-the-cuff remark that would change my life. He simply said, "After all, the Holy Spirit is our teacher." I left the pastor's study confident that I could trust the Spirit of truth to guide me into all truth (John 16:13). The Spirit himself would be my ultimate teacher! Since then, I cannot count the number of times in my preaching and teaching ministry that I have reminded my hearers that the Holy Spirit is our teacher, that his textbook is the Bible, that our whole life experience is his classroom— and that there are pop quizzes!

Witness

Jesus' next saying moves from the classroom to the courtroom. John's gospel highlights the conflict Jesus often had with the Jewish leaders. He was, in effect, constantly on trial both before his Jewish opponents and before the whole world. Jesus had already mentioned five witnesses on his behalf (John 5:31–47)—the Father, John the Baptist, Jesus own works, the Scriptures, and Moses (see previous chapter)—to which he now adds two more, to bring the total to seven, one of John's favorite numbers! "When the Advocate comes, whom I will send to you from

---

11   Moody, Spirit of the Living God, 167.

the Father—the Spirit of truth who goes out from the Father—he will testify about me. And you also must testify, for you have been with me from the beginning" (John 15:26–27). Thus, the two new witnesses are the Holy Spirit himself and—us!

First, we again note the Trinitarian reality Jesus highlights: The Paraclete is sent by Jesus from the Father and he proceeds from ("goes out from") the Father. The Spirit comes to testify to Jesus, to bear witness as in a courtroom. We, in turn, also bear witness. Later Jesus promised that the Holy Spirit would *empower* our witness. On Easter Sunday night Jesus spoke of the disciples being "witnesses of these things" and of their being "clothed with power from on high" (Luke 24:48–49). And before he ascended Jesus promised, "But you will receive power when the Holy Spirit comes on you; and you will be my witnesses" (Acts 1:8). So in this Paraclete saying Jesus is reminding us of the crucial role the Holy Spirit plays in the church's witness to Jesus.

I once heard D. James Kennedy explain at a Billy Graham School of Evangelism that witnessing was like driving rivets into the side of a boat. The rivet is held up to the side and a pneumatic hammer drives it into the hull. In witnessing, we simply lift up Christ in the gospel presentation and the Holy Spirit (*pneuma* means breath, wind, or spirit in the New Testament!) drives the truth into the heart of our hearers. It is the witness of the Spirit that is all important! We ultimately come to a confident faith in God and his Word through the witness of the Spirit. Next, we stay in the law court setting as we move to the fourth Paraclete saying, which portrays the Holy Spirit as *judge*.

Judge

Jesus makes a statement in this saying that revolutionized my Christian walk as a young man. As Jesus prepared his disciples for coming persecution and for his return to the Father, he made a comment that I found very difficult to accept, as I'm sure his disciples did as well. "But I tell you the truth, it is better for you that I go away" (John 16:7 NCV). Better? How could it be to their advantage for Jesus to leave them? Hadn't they often failed miserably in ministry when he wasn't around? And what could be better than having Jesus physically by your side? Well, there is something better, and Jesus was taking great pains to explain this revolutionary reality to them. Here is Jesus' full statement: "But very truly I tell you, it is for your good that I am going away. Unless I go away, the Advocate will not come to you, but if I go, I will send him to you" (John 16:7). Jesus was saying that having the Paraclete, the Holy Spirit, in us is better than having Jesus physically with us. In other words, having Christ *in* you 24/7 is infinitely better than having him physically *with* you. It is this spiritual union with Christ through the Holy Spirit that transforms a person's life.

Then Jesus adds:

> When he [the Paraclete] comes he will prove the world to be in the wrong about sin and righteousness and judgment: about sin, because people do not believe in me; about righteousness, because I am going to the Father, where you can see me no longer; and about judgment because the prince of this world now stands condemned (vv. 8–11).

The phrase "prove the world to be in the wrong" translates a single Greek verb meaning to "convince" or "convict." A Roman judge of that day would cross-examine the accused three times, as did Pilate in Jesus' trial (John 18:33; 19:1, 9).[12] So now the Holy Spirit stands in judgment over this wicked, rebellious world! He deals with the world concerning three things: sin, righteousness, and judgment. And all three of these things relate in one way or another back to Jesus himself. First, sin: "because

---

12   See Moody, *Spirit of the Living God,* 172.

people do not believe in me." In its essence sin is simply *unbelief.* The fatal sin of fallen humanity is not believing in Jesus.

Jesus is the number one issue of our day. And frankly I'm a little weary of clerics sitting across from a Larry King and equivocating about Jesus. King asks, "Are

> Jesus is the number one issue of our day.

you saying that if I don't believe in Jesus that I'm going to hell?" Usually, the preacher's softened response is something like "Well, I'm not the judge, Larry." That's true enough, but it's not the issue. Jesus is the issue. My response would be something like this: "Yes, Larry. Not believing in Jesus is the fatal sin of humanity. It results in eternal death. But your problem is not with me, Larry. Your problem is with Jesus himself. *He's* the one who said, "I am the way and the truth and the life. No one comes to the Father except through me" (John 14:6). I didn't say that. Jesus did. I'm just sales. He's management. Take it up with him!" We need to make Jesus the issue again. When we don't, we grieve the Holy Spirit.

Second, the Spirit deals with lost humanity about righteousness, because we can't see Jesus. He is "the Righteous One" (1 John 2:1). He is the standard of righteousness. The Spirit will draw our eyes to Jesus and prove to us our need of his atoning death for our sins, our unrighteousness. Then finally, the Spirit warns the lost about judgment. As the Spirit cross-examines us, we become poignantly aware that Satan is the ruler of this present evil age (kosmos) and that our only hope as we face the final judgment is Jesus. The good news is that for those of us who are in Christ there is no condemnation (Rom. 8:1); our sins have already been judged on the cross of Christ!

Guide

The final Paraclete saying portrays the Holy Spirit as our guide. Having a personal guide is a wonderful blessing. I have colleagues on the faculty where I serve who have lived in Israel and taken countless trips to the Holy Land. They have a facility with both biblical and modern Hebrew and a strong grasp of the history and politics of the region. They serve as wonderful guides on a Holy Land trip! The Holy Spirit is our guide throughout our entire earthly pilgrimage. Here is how Jesus taught this truth:

> I have much more to say to you, more than you can now bear. But when he, the Spirit of truth, comes, he will guide you into all the truth. He will not speak on his own; he will speak only what he hears, and he will tell you what is yet to come. He will glorify me because it is from me that he will receive what he will make known to you. All that belongs to the Father is mine. That is why I said the Spirit will receive from me what he will make known to you (John 16:12–15).

Jesus has much more to say to us. And the Holy Spirit, the Spirit of truth, wants to guide us into all the truth. Again, notice the Trinitarian context: the Spirit speaking and revealing what he hears, what he receives from Jesus, which all belongs to the Father. The Paraclete helps us make sense of our past, present, and future. He girds us for the future and glorifies the Savior in and through our lives. Could we ask for anything more!

The Personal, Divine Spirit

It has already become abundantly clear from Jesus' own teachings that the Holy Spirit is a Person and not merely an impersonal power. He is all-powerful as we will note further below, but he is a Person who can be grieved (Eph. 4:30), who can be lied to (Acts 5:3), and who "searches all things, even the deep things of God," knowing "the thoughts of God" (1 Cor. 2:10–11). He guided the early church on her worldwide mission, often speaking decisively in his directions (Acts 8:29; 10:19; 11:12; 13:2). He has a profound intercessory ministry on our behalf (Rom. 8:26–27). He is also clearly divine.

We baptize "in the name of the Father and of the Son and of the Holy Spirit" (Matt. 28:19). The Spirit gave us the Scriptures (2 Tim. 3:16; 2 Peter 1:21). Lying to the Holy Spirit means lying to God—and can shorten your life (Acts 5:3–4)! He is "the eternal Spirit" (Heb. 9:14). He sovereignly "determines" how he will "distribute" the spiritual gifts (1 Cor. 12:11). He plays a key role in the Trinity in God's sovereign work of salvation: "God the Father chose you because of what he knew beforehand. He chose you through the Holy Spirit's work of making you holy and because of the faithful obedience and sacrifice of Jesus Christ" (1 Peter 1:2 CEB). And as the executive in charge of directing the church on her end time mission, he continues to reign supreme. One of the greatest indications of the deity of the Spirit is his role in creation.

The Creator Spirit

We first encounter the Holy Spirit in the biblical narrative "in the beginning," at the creation of the cosmos:

> In the beginning God created the heavens and the earth. Now the earth was formless and empty, darkness was over the surface of the deep, and the Spirit of God was hovering over the waters. And God said . . ." (Gen. 1:1–3).

Already we see a preparation for the doctrine of the Trinity with the references to (1) God, (2) the Spirit of God, and (3) the Word of God ("And God said"; see John 1:1–3). Even the name for God here, *Elohim*, is plural, but with a singular verb, another preparation for a triune concept of deity. And the portrait of the Spirit in these opening words of the Bible is dynamic.

The word for "Spirit" is *ruach*, a vivid reference to wind, breath, or spirit. The mighty *action* of the Spirit of God is also striking: He hovers over the dark, chaotic waters like a mother-bird protecting and providing for her young, like an eagle teaching her young to fly (see Deut. 32:10–11). "God's Spirit brooded like a bird above the watery abyss" (Gen. 1:2 *The Message*). But the powerful action of the Spirit is also seen in the ongoing creation down to our own day. Psalm 104, a hymnic celebration of the Creator, refers to the action of God's Spirit in bringing forth all earth's creatures: "When you send your Spirit, they are created, and you renew the face of the ground" (v. 30). Elihu, in the book of Job, says, "The Spirit of God has made me; the breath of the Almighty gives me life" (Job 33:4). In other words, the Holy Spirit is God. He created all things and he created *you*. And the Bible uses graphic metaphors for the Spirit.

Wind, Fire, Water, Dove

"When the day of Pentecost came, they were all together in one place. Suddenly a sound like the blowing of a violent wind came from heaven and filled the whole house where they were sitting" (Acts 2:1–2). Wind is one of my favorite metaphors for the Holy Spirit. I grew up in West Texas, where the wind is virtually incessant. I have lived much of my life in Oklahoma, "where the wind comes sweeping down the plain." I lived by the ocean in Florida for awhile and have vivid memories of sitting on the dock watching the wind move the waters. So I can relate to the Bible's use of this metaphor in relation to the Holy Spirit! Jesus told Nicodemus that the new birth was mysterious like the wind: "The wind blows wherever it pleases. You hear its sound, but you cannot tell where it comes from or where it is going. So it is with everyone born of the Spirit" (John 3:8). Wind powerfully depicts the action of God's Spirit in our lives.

Wind can be quiet and refreshing. It can also be violent and intrusive. The breezes off the ocean kept our house in Florida cool and refreshed.

But I have also seen the wind whip up massive waves as a tropical storm hovered nearby. In the yard of our Oklahoma home we lost a beautiful Bradford Pear tree to a freak seventy-mile-an-hour wind. And the twisters of this region are notorious. The Spirit works in similar ways. He most often speaks in a still, small voice. But he can show up surprisingly and powerfully. "Pentecost was a sudden, sovereign action of God right out of heaven!"[13] The past century and the opening years of the new millennium have witnessed the greatest revival of the church's history, with the global explosion of Pentecostalism. To say the least, this sovereign outpouring has often been disconcerting to sleepy, safe American Christendom.

William H. Willimon, in a chapel sermon at Duke University, depicted well this provocative nature of the Spirit's intrusive ways:

> All evidence to the contrary, we continue to sin against Pentecost, continue to attempt to explain away the disruptive descent of the Spirit. And you know why. The Acts 2 threat that one Sunday we might all gather here in our bolted down pews, with our smug reasonableness, our bourgeois respectability, only to be grabbed by our collective collar, shaken up, thrown into confusion, intoxicated, is not a suggestion we welcome. Most of us come in here to be confirmed in what we think we already know; not to be dislodged, led by the Spirit into *terra incognita* we do not know. But be careful. As you come to the table today, with hands open, maybe even minds open, be careful. The wind blows where it will (John 3), God's Spirit will not be housebroken by us, and your soul might catch fire, even yet, even here.
>
> I would hate to see nice, respectable people like you with mortgages go out of here *drunk*.
>
> No I wouldn't.[14]

---

13 Larry D. Hart, *Truth Aflame: Theology for the Church in Renewal*, rev. ed. (Grand Rapids: Zondervan, 2005), 381.

14 William H. Willimon, *"They're Drunk,"* Pentecost Sermon, Duke University Chapel, May 22, 1994 (transcipt), pp. 3–4. (Willimon's italics).

Willimon mentions *fire*—another great metaphor for the Spirit!

At Pentecost "they saw what seemed to be tongues of fire that separated and came to rest on each of them" (Acts 2:4). The apostle Paul exhorted young Timothy to "fan into flame the gift of God, which is in you through the laying on of my hands. For the Spirit God gave us does not make us timid, but gives us power, love and self-discipline" (2 Tim. 1:6–7). He warned the Thessalonians: "Do not quench the Spirit" (1 Thess. 5:19), that is, don't put out the fire! And to the Romans Paul wrote: "Don't hesitate to be enthusiastic—be on fire in the Spirit as you serve the Lord!" (Rom. 12:11 CEB). The world needs to see the church ablaze with the Spirit yet again! Surely we should pray to that end. And Pentecost is the paradigm.

Peter explained the descent of the Spirit at Pentecost as a fulfillment of Joel's prophecy: "In the last days, God says, I will pour out my Spirit on all people" (Acts 2:17; Joel 2:28). Here water is the controlling metaphor. The prophets predicted an outpouring of the Holy Spirit in the Messianic age: "till the Spirit is poured on us from on high" (Isa. 32:15); "I will pour out my Spirit on your offspring" (Isa. 44:3); "I will pour out my Spirit on the people of Israel" (Ez. 39:29; see also Zech. 12:10–13:1). We will see later how the apostle John will pick up on this picture of the effusion of God's Spirit. God's pouring out the water of the Spirit is one of the most appealing pictures of our salvation in the Bible.

The final image we will consider is the dove, probably the best known symbol for the Holy Spirit. It takes us back to the beginnings of Jesus' public ministry, when Jesus was baptized by the John the Baptist: "When all the people were being baptized, Jesus was baptized too. And as he was praying, heaven was opened and the Holy Spirit descended on him in bodily form like a dove. And a voice came from heaven: 'You are my Son, whom I love; with you I am well pleased'" (Luke 3:21–22). This is one of the greatest revelations of the Trinity in the Scriptures. The Spirit descends and the Father speaks, announcing the Son of his love. We have another bird-metaphor here similar to the creation account (Gen. 1:2).

Luke's language in this account emphasizes the objective nature of the Spirit's descent upon Jesus. "In bodily form like a dove" (Luke 3:22), similar to the tongues of fire at Pentecost (Acts 2:3–4), points to a reality created by God himself and not merely an internal human thought or feeling. This was a concrete manifestation of the Holy Spirit himself.[15] In both instances, Jesus' baptism and Pentecost, we are witnessing an empowerment event.

> For Jesus, the Spirit comes to empower him for his ministry. In this sense, he is no different from the disciples in Acts and serves as a model for them. Prayer and the Holy Spirit unleash the power of God in their lives to engage in their mission effectively (see Acts 1:14; 2:3–4).[16]

Much more will be said about the Spirit's empowering work (and prayer) later.

Wind, fire, water, dove—all images which can connote either gentle or vigorous action on the part of the Holy Spirit. He moves in ways that he sovereignly determines. He cannot be controlled. He cannot be manipulated. His timing is impeccable. He knows just how and when to show up and often shake things up! Our next task, then, is to examine in-depth the wonderful, powerful work of the Holy Spirit, to explore the fundamental ways God wants to work in us.

He moves in ways that he sovereignly determines. He cannot be controlled. He cannot be manipulated.

15 David E. Garland, *Exegetical Commentary on the New Testament: Luke* (Grand Rapids: Zondervan, 2011), 168-169.
16 Garland, *Luke,* 169.

HOW
GOD
WORKS
IN US

CHAPTER FOUR
GOD'S PASCHAL WORK

The wave of the future in almost every field of study is learning to think *dimensionally*. After thousands of years of human civilization with its newest prodigy being science, we are finally catching up to what the Bible has been teaching us all along—that there are dimensions beyond our four dimensional cosmos of space and time. We now know we live in a multi-dimensional universe, and we are only beginning to unveil what that actually means. Astronomer Hugh Ross has expressed this well:

> The wave of the future in almost every field of study is learning to think *dimensionally.*

> A few thousand years before physicists conceived of general relativity, the space-time theorem, quarks, supersymmetry, unified field theories, and vibrating strings, a written document described extra-dimensional reality. That document is the Bible. . . . no other book previous to the modern era describes phenomena in dimensions independent of our four.[1]

Christian theologians have actually been a little slow in picking up on the implications of the discoveries of astronomers and physicists. I'm convinced that many of our "sticking points" in terms of coming

---

1   Hugh Ross, *Beyond the Cosmos* (Colorado Springs, CO: NavPress, 1996), 41

to a consensus on certain doctrines would dissolve if we took a dimensional approach. Never is this truer than in relation to the work of the Holy Spirit. Thinking dimensionally enables us simultaneously to see the wholeness of things while noting intricate complexities and diversities.

Here is a prime example of what I'm talking about: What did John the Baptist mean when he made the following announcement? "I baptize you with water for repentance. But after me comes one who is more powerful than I, whose sandals I am not worthy to carry. He will baptize you with the Holy Spirit and fire" (Matt. 3:11). What is this Spirit baptism that John was referring to? Three typical responses are (1) that John is referring to the new birth or (2) to the Spirit's sanctifying work, or (3) that he is saying that Jesus will empower us for our mission. This is a crass simplification of these important doctrinal debates and it can be argued that each camp has made valuable contributions to our understanding of the Christian life and mission. But our next step of inquiry will be in large measure to find out just what John the Baptist was actually talking about.

We've looked at who God is. Now we want to explore how God works *in* us. (Later we will examine how God wants to work *through* us.) I see the work of God's Spirit in our lives as having three fundamental dimensions, according to the Scriptures. Again, this is Christianity in 3D! Could John the Baptist's announcement of Jesus' Spirit-and-fire baptism actually have been a programmatic description of Jesus' entire end time work of salvation, including Christian initiation, the Christian life, and empowerment for Christian mission? In other words, we've missed it by asking Is it A, B, or C? No, it's D, all of the above! The three dimensions of the Spirit's work in our lives I have termed Paschal, Purifying, and Pentecostal.

In this chapter we will explore the greatest miracle any human being can ever experience. It involves an actual multi-dimensional transformation of our lives that impacts us for all eternity! Yes, we have to introduce the concept of miracle to get at this reality. Unless you're willing to expand your mind to consider the possibility of such an extra-dimensional phenomenon, you will simply be unable to assimilate what the Bible is referring to here. Next we will examine how God's work of transforming us transitions into a lifelong experience of renewal and change. Then, we will explore the power that God has made available to us so that we can share all this good news and serve others effectively.

Why have I chosen such arcane terms as Paschal, Purifying, and Pentecostal to refer to these fundamental dimensions of the work of the Holy Spirit? Well, for one thing, I am an ordained Southern Baptist preacher and professor and we Baptists simply *love* alliteration! Also, I am a professional theologian and we scholars tend to lean toward a somewhat exalted vocabulary because it makes us feel smarter. (Actually, we use such terms as a sort of professional shorthand, saying a whole lot with one word or phrase.) I could use other terms to refer to these three fundamental dimensions of the Spirit's work such as "salvation, sanctification, and service," "conversion, consecration, and charisma," or, simply, "how to get started, straight, and strong." But even some of these words are foreign to many, so I'll stick with the three P's.[2]

Thinking dimensionally enables us to guard the *unity* of truth. There is one Holy Spirit. Therefore, there is only one work of the Holy Spirit and it is whatever the Holy Spirit does! But clearly there are three fundamental dimensions to his one work. When the Holy Spirit comes into our lives, all three dimensions of his work are present—because he is

---

2 I have previously published treatments of the three-dimensional work of the Holy Spirit in the following volumes: *Truth Aflame: Theology for the Church in Renewal* (Grand Rapids: Zondervan, 2005), 388–404; "Spirit Baptism: A Dimensional Charismatic Perspective" in *Perspectives on Spirit Baptism: Five Views*, ed. Chad Owen Brand (Nashville: B & H Publishers, 2004), 105–169; and "Spirit Baptism: A Bridge-Building Biblical Metaphor for All Churches and All Generations" in *Spirit-Empowered Christianity in the 21st Century*, gen. ed., Vinson Synan (Lake Mary, Fl.: Charisma House, 2011), 261–286. I will be drawing on these resources in the presentation that follows.

present! We are going to spend the rest of this chapter and the next two chapters unwrapping just what this means. We will be exploring some of the most liberating truths of the Scriptures.

It also seems clear that God has providentially provided a specific New Testament author to emphasize and explicate each of the three dimensions of the Spirit's work. John underscores the Paschal dimension, showing how the Spirit brings us into a new birth and into eternal life. Paul explains how the Spirit enables us to live holy lives. And Luke focuses almost entirely on the empowering dimension of the Spirit's work. So this chapter focuses primarily on John's writings in the New Testament and the following two chapters will give a hearing to Paul and Luke respectively.

> 3D Christianity is about what God is doing, not us!

3D Christianity entails fully embracing all three dimensions of the Spirit's work in our lives. God wants to make us rich in his love, joy, peace, patience, kindness, goodness, faithfulness, gentleness, and self-control (Gal. 5:22). He also wants to use different ones of us in words of wisdom, words of knowledge, faith, healings, miracles, prophecies, discerning of spirits, tongues, interpretation of tongues, serving, teaching, encouraging, giving, leading, and showing mercy (1 Cor. 12:8–10; Rom. 12:6–8), as well as even gifting some of us to live a celibate life (1 Cor. 7:7). And these are not exhaustive listings of spiritual gifts, but merely suggestive and descriptive indications of ways in which the Spirit works. 3D Christianity is about what *God* is doing, not us! And it all begins with a new birth.

Behold, the Lamb of God!

John wants us to discover 3D Christianity as a new life, an eternal life, in Jesus Christ. His explicitly stated purpose for his gospel is that we "may believe that Jesus is the Messiah, the Son of God, and that by believing [we] may have life in his name" (John 20:31). The words of John the Baptist set the pace for the entire narrative: "Behold, the Lamb of God, who takes away the sin of the world!" (John 1:29 ESV). Jesus is *God's* lamb. As the apostle Paul wrote, "Christ, our pas-

> John wants us to discover 3D Christianity as a new life, an eternal life, in Jesus Christ.

chal lamb, has been sacrificed" (1 Cor. 5:7 RSV). And as Abraham said to Isaac, "God himself will provide the lamb" (Gen. 22:8). Isaiah prophesied that Jesus would be "led like a lamb to the slaughter" (Isa. 53:7). So Jesus himself came as the paschal, or Passover, lamb for the sins of humanity.

John the Baptist adds additional comments that serve, along with the Passion Narrative of John's gospel, as brackets, or bookends, for the entire book:

> The next day John saw Jesus coming toward him and said, "Behold, the Lamb of God, who takes away the sin of the world! This is he of whom I said, "After me comes a man who ranks before me, because he was before me. I myself did not know him, but for this purpose I came baptizing with water, that he might be revealed to Israel." And John bore witness: "I saw the Spirit descend from heaven like a dove, and it remained on him. I myself did not know him, but he who sent me to baptize with water said to me, 'He on whom you see the Spirit descend and remain, this is he who baptizes with the Holy Spirit.' And I have seen and have borne witness that this is the Son of God" (John 1:29–34 ESV).

The two key names to note are "the Lamb of God, who takes away the sin of the world" and "he who baptizes with the Holy Spirit."

John's account of the death of Jesus contains some details and emphases not found in the other gospels. Only John tells us that when the soldiers came to break Jesus' legs but chose not to because he was already dead, that "one of the soldiers pierced Jesus' side with a spear, bringing a sudden flow of blood and water" (John 19:33–34). In the following verses, John puts even more emphasis on the fact that his testimony to this event is factual. Why was the sudden flow of blood and water so important to John? A passage in 1 John answers this question directly:

> Water and blood came out from the side of Jesus Christ. It wasn't just water, but water and blood. The Spirit tells about this, because the Spirit is truthful. In fact, there are three who tell about it. They are the Spirit, the water, and the blood, and they all agree (1 John 5:6–8 CEV).

In simplest terms, here was John's message: (1) Blood: "Behold, the Lamb of God, who takes away the sin of the world!" (2) Water: "this is he who baptizes with the Holy Spirit." Then follows the culmination, "this is the Son of God."

Gary Burge, a specialist in Johannine studies, observes that John 19:34 and 1 John 5:6–8 "are conceptually in the same school: blood, water, testimony, and the Spirit all converge"—the latter passage addresses who Jesus *is*, in the face of the distorted doctrines (heresies) of the day, while the former passage stresses what Jesus has *done* for us in his atonement for our sins.[3] And the Spirit's role is crucial in all of this. It is only through what the Holy Spirit does that we are able to enter the eternal life Jesus has made available to us. Throughout the entire narrative of John's gospel, the Spirit's role is emphasized.

Perhaps John's most familiar story is that of Nicodemus, whom Jesus taught the true significance of salvation in the kingdom of God. Inductively, Nicodemus had concluded that Jesus must be "a teacher

---

3 Gary M. Burge, *The Anointed Community: The Holy Spirit in the Johannine Tradition* (Grand Rapids: Eerdmans, 1987), 95.

who has come from God. For no one could perform the signs you are doing if God were not with him" (John 3:2). But Jesus doesn't commend Nicodemus for his accurate reasoning. Rather he warns Nicodemus, a teacher of Israel, that unless he has a new birth, he will never see nor enter God's kingdom: "Very truly I tell you, no one can see the kingdom of God unless they are born again" (v. 3). The word "again" (*anothen*) can be translated "again" or "from above." Both translations work in the context and they are not mutually exclusive. Entrance into God's kingdom requires a second birth from above—a birth wrought by the Spirit of God.

Jesus uses two metaphors for the Holy Spirit and his work in our lives in his conversation with Nicodemus: water and wind. Nicodemus was thinking only in natural terms in relation to this new birth, while Jesus was pointing him heavenward to the Spirit's mighty saving actions.

> Jesus answered, "Very truly I tell you, no one can enter the kingdom of God unless they are born of water and the Spirit. Flesh gives birth to flesh, but the Spirit gives birth to spirit. You should not be surprised at my saying, 'You must be born again.' The wind blows wherever it pleases. You hear its sound, but you cannot tell where it comes from or where it is going. So it is with everyone born of the Spirit" (John 3:5–8).

The phrase, "born of water and the Spirit," is very likely what Greek scholars would call a hendiadys, that is, one preposition governing two nouns (water and Spirit). So the translation would then run "born of the water of the Spirit" and would be another reference to Spirit baptism. Jesus will use the same water metaphor for the Spirit later in this gospel.

Then Jesus describes the mysterious work of the Spirit in the new birth as being like the wind. The words "wind" and "Spirit" are the same Greek term, *pneuma*. So now the Spirit is depicted as being like the wind: We can't tell where the wind is coming from or where it is going! So it is with the way the Spirit works in our lives. It is always encouraging to hear someone's testimony. Each unique story points to the mysterious and unpredictable ways the Spirit moves in a person's life.

My mother was born again on October 13, 1946. About three months later, she found out I was on the way, and she and my father dedicated me to the Lord. I was born on October 13, 1947, the one year anniversary of her spiritual birth! And from my earliest memories I always had a drive to know God. His Spirit began convicting me of sin when I was only six years old, and I was born again at seven. Looking back, I can only attribute this to the mysterious moving of the Spirit. The wind "blows wherever it pleases," and I was "born of the water of the Spirit"! Next, Jesus would explain this greatest of all miracles to a Samaritan woman at Jacob's well at Sychar.

Jesus always knew exactly how to reach a person. He was sitting by this famous well in Sychar at noon, when a woman came to draw water. Her timing clearly indicated that she was a social outcast. And it was also clear that Jesus, a Jewish man, should not be striking up a conversation with this Samaritan woman with a sullied reputation. He began by asking her for her help. He asked her for a drink of water. Here comes one of John's favorite themes again. Water is everywhere in his gospel: the Jordan where John was baptizing in chapter one, the ceremonial water pots at the wedding in Cana in chapter two, the Pool of Bethesda in chapter five, and the Pool of Siloam in chapter seven. Actually, Nicodemus may have been thinking of the waters of proselyte baptism, where a Gentile might experience cleansing and a "new birth" into Judaism, when Jesus mentioned the water of the Spirit (chapter three). So Jesus initiates the interview with the mention of water.

Immediately, the Samaritan woman points up the impropriety of Jesus' conversational gesture. But Jesus responds: "If you knew the gift of God and who it is that asks you for a drink, you would have asked him and he would have given you living water" (John 4:10). Later Jesus would add that the water he was offering would become in her "a spring of water welling up to eternal life" (v. 14). There is much more to the story, but the final outcome went like this: "Then, leaving her water jar, the woman went back to the town and said to the people, 'Come, see a man who told me everything I ever did. Could this be the Messiah?'" (vv. 28–29). This woman's life had been changed by Jesus.

Earlier in the conversation, the Samaritan woman introduced the topic of appropriate worship—broaching the subject of the Jew/Samaritan divide as a sort of diversion from the real issues. Jesus responded by asserting two things: (1) "salvation is from the Jews" and (2) "God is spirit, and his worshipers must worship in the Spirit and in truth." "True worshipers will worship the Father in the Spirit and in truth, for they are the kind of worshipers the Father seeks" (vv. 22–24). This is 3D Christianity, an authentic relationship with the Father—through Jesus, in the Spirit. And it all starts when Jesus gives us a drink, the living waters of the Spirit!

> This is 3D Christianity, an authentic relationship with the Father—through Jesus, in the Spirit.

Jesus, the baptizer in the Spirit, is the source of eternal life. "God has given us eternal life, and this life is in his Son. Whoever has the Son has life; whoever does not have the Son of God does not have life" (1 John 5:11–12). And Jesus alone is the source of the rivers of living water. That's why Christians should never be shy about making Jesus the issue. There is no one else to go to if we want eternal life. He alone is "the way and the truth and the life. No one comes to the Father except through

[him]" (John 14:6). Jesus made this publically clear later at the Festival of Tabernacles in Jerusalem.

Only months before Jesus would go to Calvary, he entered Jerusalem quietly during the Fall Festival of Tabernacles (John 7). Everyone was looking for him, including those who were plotting his death. Earlier his own brothers had shown that even they did not believe in him. Jesus waited until the culminating day of the festival, which involved a solemn procession from the Pool of Siloam with water jars to be poured forth on the temple mount while the promises of the prophets of an end time outpouring of God's Spirit were recited.

Jesus stood forth and proclaimed in a loud voice:

> Let anyone who is thirsty come to me!
> Let any one who believes in me come and drink!
> (John 7:37 NJB)

John adds, "By this he meant the Spirit, whom those who believed in him were later to receive" (v. 39). Jesus was announcing that he himself was the source of the "rivers of living water" (v. 38). One could also take Jesus' words as referring to rivers flowing from within believers. Both ideas could be taken together!

These words are fulfilled in John's gospel on Easter Sunday night. Jesus appeared to ten of his disciples, breathed on them, and said, "Receive the Holy Spirit" (John 20:22). His words echoed the creation narrative in which God took the dust of the earth, breathed in the breath of life, "and the man became a living being" (Gen. 2:7). Jesus was starting a whole new humanity! This was the culmination of John's portrayal of Jesus' saving work on our behalf, made real and personally applicable by the impartation of the Spirit.

The work of the Holy Spirit, then, in John's writings, brings about a new birth in the Spirit. It entails receiving eternal life here and now!

And it all relates to Calvary. 3D Christianity involves the work of the Father, the Son, and the Holy Spirit. The Father initiates it all. The Son makes it all available through his saving death and resurrection. And the Spirit applies personally this saving work in the believer's life. It is what scholars would call a cross-centered pneumatology (doctrine of the Holy Spirit). Gary Burge provides these wise guiding comments:

> Finally, this dual message of John—that the Spirit is released through the cross and that Christ and Spirit must never be separated—has an important contemporary relevance. Any theology which separates salvation from the life-creating Spirit is inadequate (contra many "second-blessing" theologies). Any theology which separates the acceptance of Jesus from the gift of the Spirit is incorrect. Our experience of the Spirit is wrapped up in our experience of Christ's sacrifice on the cross. Similarly, the anchor for unbounded enthusiasm must be the glorification of the historical person of Jesus.[4]

Finally, on that same Easter Sunday night, Jesus made it crystal clear that this wonderful gift of the Spirit was not meant only for one's private benefit. Before he imparted the Spirit he announced, "As the Father has sent me, I am sending you" (John 20:21). Throughout John's gospel, Jesus makes reference to his being sent by the Father. Now he is sending out his disciples with this same good news—Jesus can give you living water, which will become in you an artesian well springing up to eternal life!

---

4 Burge, *The Anointed Community*, 149.

CHAPTER FIVE
GOD'S PURIFYING WORK

It is extremely easy in our day to allow the world to eclipse God. We are saturated with naturalism. Factoring out the rampant cruelty and evil across this planet as well as hints of the mysterious and transcendent, most of us seem to be content to grasp at all the dazzling pleasures that surround us. I just got a new computer while writing this book, and there's plenty packed into my new toy to keep me entertained for hours on end. I am on a sabbatical leave from my teaching post in a seminary as I write these words, and my wife and I have some exciting and exotic travel plans in the offing for the next six months. There's a great big, enticing world out there for us to explore! Rodney Reeves asks the right questions in the face of these captivating realities:

> Why would God make the world so good, so desirable, and then expect us to deny ourselves of these things that bring such basic pleasure? Why would God engineer sex to feel so good and then tell us, "Ah, ah, ah, Don't do it"? Why would he make us to feel so satisfied after we've stuffed ourselves with more food than we need? . . . Our bodies seem to be geared for greed. We always want more. Looking forward to dessert seems eschatological. Smacking our lips always breeds a smile.[1]

---

1 Rodney Reeves, *Spirituality According to Paul* (Downers Grove, Ill.: IVP Academic, 2011),55.

Without our realizing it, the actual problem we're wrestling with here is sin—yes, I actually wrote the "s" word so taboo in our day—SIN! And the Bible's answer to this ubiquitous problem for humanity is singular: CHRIST.

> How is sin conquered in our lives? How do we live holy lives? Where is the help and power that we so desperately need? The answer to these questions is singular: THE HOLY SPIRIT.

Most believers acknowledge these realities. They acknowledge the tragedy of sin and the necessity of Christ's remedy on the cross. What too often is missing, however, is precisely how that atoning death liberates us from the downward pull of sin we all experience. How is sin conquered in our lives? How do we live holy lives? Where is the help and power that we so desperately need? And the answer to these questions is also singular: THE HOLY SPIRIT.

There is no better place to turn in the Scriptures for how this works than to the writings of the apostle Paul. Paul clearly deals with the regenerating and empowering dimensions of the Spirit's work. But taken as a whole, there is a much greater emphasis in his writings on the Spirit's empowering us to live holy lives. In one of his earliest letters, the apostle states forthrightly, "this is the will of God, your sanctification [or holiness, *hagiasmos*]" (1 Thess. 4:3 NRSV). He was writing them about a life that is pleasing to God, a life, for example, of sexual purity in which we control our bodies in "holiness [*hagiasmos*] and honor" (v. 4), adding that God "did not call us to impurity but in holiness [*hagiasmos*] (v. 7). Then to sum it all up he announces, "Therefore, anyone who rejects this instruction does not reject a human being but God, the very God who gives you his Holy Spirit" (v. 8). The word order here in the original emphasizes "Holy," signifying the following: The proof positive that God intends you to live a holy life is the fact that he has given you his *Holy* Spirit!

Paul develops this same theme of a call to holiness in his first letter to those carnal Corinthians. He reminded them of the sinful lives out of which God had called them to salvation. Then he adds, "But you were washed, you were sanctified, you were justified in the name of the Lord Jesus Christ and by the Spirit of our God" (1 Cor. 6:11). He puts it all together here! The Holy Spirit is the one who washes us, sanctifies us, and justifies us "in the name of the Lord Jesus Christ." His reminder of their past spiritual transformation is used as a call to *present* holiness, and it all comes about ultimately because of Jesus' death and resurrection.[2]

But Paul provides his most complete explanation of precisely how the Holy Spirit enables us to live holy lives in Romans and Galatians. Romans is Paul's most complete presentation of the gospel. It is sort of his systematic theology. In fact, I have often remarked in my theology classes that if I only had this epistle as the class text, I could very easily teach the entirety of systematic theology. With Galatians we have Paul's spirited *defense* of the gospel. In the process, he emphasizes the Spirit's role in applying the gospel's liberating power in our daily living and personal relations. Both letters, Romans and Galatians, complement each other to provide a full-orbed presentation of the liberating gospel of Jesus Christ.

I have sometimes begun a sermon or class by asking my hearers to "turn with me please to 'The Gospel According to Paul.'" There is usually a long pause, with puzzled looks my way, before I add "the Book of Romans." But this epistle does fully display God's Good News for all humanity in a very systematic manner. Paul announces:

> For I am not ashamed of the gospel, because it is the power
> of God that brings salvation to everyone who believes: first to
> the Jew, then to the Gentile. For in the gospel the righteousness
> of God is revealed—a righteousness that is by faith from first

---

2 Gordon D. Fee, *God's Empowering Presence: The Holy Spirit in the Letters of Paul* (Peabody, Mass.: Hendrickson, 1994), 127-132.

to last, just as it is written: "The righteous will live by faith" (Rom. 1:16–17).

But then the apostle immediately adds, "For the wrath of God is revealed from heaven against all ungodliness and wickedness of those who by their wickedness suppress the truth" (v. 18 NRSV). Two revelations: (1) the righteousness of God, which points to God's saving action; and (2) the wrath of God, which points to God's judgment. Actually, in the gospel, we have one revelation with two dimensions: judgment and salvation. God judges our sin at Calvary while simultaneously offering us salvation from sin. But sin is the issue. It is the cause of all the misery of humanity. It is why we cannot have enough psychiatrists, policemen, lawyers, or preachers. So for the next couple of chapters, Paul provides an x-ray analysis of this universal problem of sin (Rom. 1:18–3:20).

Then with one paragraph-long sentence (in the original—we have to break it up into separate sentences when we translate it), Paul summarizes his whole gospel presentation (Rom. 3:21–26). Here the apostle speaks again of God's righteousness, which he gives to us as a gift, by his grace, through Christ's atoning sacrifice—all of which we receive by faith. Then follows further explication and explanation of these astounding realities (Rom. 3:27–5:21). This is truth with profound relevance for the plight of all humankind. Every person, every nation, every culture needs to know this good news. We all have the same problem: sin. And there is only one solution: Jesus Christ. No one else. Period. But Paul is not through. He is eager to show how Christ's death liberates us from our literal enslavement to sin. That will be the subject of the next three chapters (Rom. 6–8). Jesus died, was buried, and rose again, Paul argues, that we might live a transformed life.[3]

---

3   The discussion that follows is taken from my previously published comments on this subject: "Spirit Baptism: A Dimensional Charismatic Perspective" in *Perspectives on Spirit Baptism: Five Views* (Nashvile: B & H Publishers, 2004), 137-139.

Chapter six of Romans shows how our identification with Christ's death and resurrection liberates us from sin. We die to sin with Christ to walk in newness of life as slaves of righteousness, which is true freedom. C. E. B. Cranfield has mastered the apostle's concept here.[4] Our death with Christ takes place in four ways, according to the apostle, and it is this fourfold sense of our identity with Christ's death that is being applied in this chapter. Paul's programmatic statement in this regard is: "one has died for all, therefore all have died" (2 Cor. 5:14). Here are the four senses: *The Juridical Sense*: By God's gracious decision, when Christ died we all died; God was beginning a whole new humanity in the person of his resurrected Son (2 Cor. 5:14; Col. 3:1–4). *The Baptismal Sense*: We died with Christ and were raised with him at our conversion (Rom. 6:1–4; Col. 2:12). *The Moral Sense*: We experience Christ's death daily as we, by the Spirit, mortify sin in our lives (the major argument of Rom. 6; 8:13; cf. 1 Cor. 15:31; 2 Cor. 1:9; 4:11, referring to Paul's suffering for the gospel). *The Eschatological Sense*: The battle with sin comes to an end with our physical death, and the resurrection completes our redemption from sin and death (Rom. 8:23).

Thus, Christ's death is central to our sanctification. Spirit baptism ultimately applies Christ's death and resurrection to bring about a transformed life. This is the purifying dimension of the Spirit's work. The next two chapters of Romans explain how this takes place.

Romans 7 transports us back to the garden where the first couple fell. Sin, like Satan, seizes the opportunity of God's commandment to deceive us and kill us (Rom. 7:7–12/Gen. 3:1–13). Consequently, we are all "sold into slavery under sin" (v. 14). We suffer from a sort of spiritual schizophrenia (vv. 14–21). Sin now has its camp in our physical bodies, preventing us from fulfilling God's law (vv. 22–25). What is the answer to this moral and spiritual dilemma? It is the cross. It is Christ. It is the Holy Spirit.

---

4   See C. E. B. Cranfield, *The Epistle to Romans*, Vol. 2, *The International Critical Commentary* (Edinburgh: T. & T. Clark, 1979), 830-33, upon which the following comments are based.

> God does for us what we could never do for ourselves.

God does for us what we could never do for ourselves. *Our sanctification is just as much a work of God's grace as our justification!* This is the culmination of Paul's teaching on the Spirit's sanctifying work (Rom. 8).

What the law of Moses could not do, because of human depravity, *God did,* sending his own Son "in the likeness of sinful flesh" and as an offering for sin, God "condemned (cf. the noun form of this verb in v. 1) in the flesh" so that we might fulfill the law by walking "according to the Spirit" (vv. 3–4). "For the law of the Spirit of life in Christ Jesus has set you free from the law of sin and of death," Paul begins (v. 2). Three laws are in purview here: (1) the Law of Moses, (2) the law of sin and death, and (3) the law of the Spirit of life in Christ Jesus. Moses' law is powerless to liberate us from the downward pull of sin. The law of sin and death, like gravity, continually pulls us downward. But the law of the Spirit of life in Christ Jesus, like the law of aerodynamics, lifts us to a new level of living! We can now live in the Spirit (v. 4) and have the mindset (*phronēma*) of the Spirit (vv. 5–8). "By the Spirit" we can put to death the evil deeds of the body (v. 13).

We were given the gift of the Holy Spirit to empower us for holy living, not just to do signs and wonders. In fact, as Paul would say elsewhere, without Christlike character, our miraculous gifts are hollow and meaningless (1 Cor. 13). The Spirit wants to liberate us from selfish, sensual, and stingy living into the freedom of a life of loving service to God and others. It is this freedom in the gospel that the apostle defends in his Galatian epistle.

The Galatian believers were being enticed by false teachers to go back under the law by requiring circumcision for salvation. But Paul would have none of it; he had already been down that road:

> You foolish Galatians! Who put a spell on you? Before your
> very eyes you had a clear description of the death of Jesus

Christ on the cross! Tell me this one thing: did you receive God's Spirit by doing what the Law requires or by hearing the gospel and believing it? How can you be so foolish? You began by God's Spirit; do you now want to finish by your own power? Did all your experience mean nothing at all? Surely it meant something! Does God give you the Spirit and work miracles among you because you do what the Law requires or because you hear the gospel and believe it? (Gal. 3:1–5 GNT).

Notice here how all three dimensions of the Spirit's work—paschal, purifying, and Pentecostal—are made available through the gospel. *The gift of the Spirit, Spirit baptism, brings with it new birth, new life, and miraculous ministry.* Only the Spirit himself can regenerate, sanctify, and empower us. And all of this has its source in the gospel of Christ, publicly portrayed as crucified.

The apostle was exhorting his readers to refuse to lose their freedom in Christ: "For freedom Christ has set us free. Stand firm, therefore, and do not submit again to a yoke of slavery" (Gal. 5:1). To receive circumcision after receiving the gospel was to cut oneself off from Christ, to fall from grace (vv. 2–4). "For through the Spirit, by faith, we eagerly wait for the hope of righteousness" (v. 5). Living in the Spirit liberates us from the bondage of sin and the destructive works of our fallen nature (vv. 16–21). Now we are free to harvest the Spirit's fruit in our lives (5:22–23; 6:7–8). "And those who belong to Christ Jesus have crucified the flesh with its passions and desires" (5:24). Again, the Spirit applies Christ's cross in our lives.

And here is Paul's bottom line: "Since we live by the Spirit, let us keep in step with the Spirit" (v. 25 NIV). The words "keep in step" translate the Greek term *stoikeō*, which is a military term: Since we have our very lives by the Spirit, we are under obligation to let him direct our lives. When we do so, we are enabled to love one another and thus fulfill the whole law (v. 14).

This was the gospel Paul defended. The "full gospel," to use a popular charismatic phrase, entails justification *and* sanctification as well as charismatic empowerment. And it is only by the power of the Spirit that we can "rightly proclaim, savingly appropriate, and effectively live out the gospel."[5] But the Pentecostals and charismatics still have a point: The Spirit *has* come "to empower us to do the same kingdom work our Lord did in his earthly ministry. And that work was in major part a charismatic work!"[6]

Much attention has been given to the paschal dimension of the Spirit's work. And because of the explosion of Pentecostal Christianity across the globe in the twentieth century and on into the new millennium, who hasn't heard about or claimed to have experienced the charismatic dimension? Unfortunately, there has been an abysmal neglect of the sanctifying work of the Spirit. Two equal and opposite errors have occurred with reference to holiness.

Some have fallen into the same trap that Jesus' opponents, the Pharisees, often embraced: legalism. Holiness by laws! Paul himself had tried that approach and found it to be a cul-de-sac. In fact, he discovered that he had become an enemy of the gospel in this mistaken approach to holiness. Legalism is the besetting sin of all revival and restoration movements. Virtually anything in the Christian life can be turned into a legalism. Prayer, Bible reading, and witnessing, can all be perverted! Have you ever been hustled by a "scalp-hunter"? You get the feeling that they're sharing with you the facts of the gospel all right, but more out of a pursuit of some kind of religious achievement than out of a genuine compassion and concern for your well-being. It's kind of like having a flower pinned on you, without being asked, by some hairless person in strange garb at an airport.

---

5 Larry D. Hart, *Truth Aflame: Theology for the Church in Renewal* (Grand Rapids: Zondervan, 2005), 347.
6 Hart, *Truth Aflame,* 351.

Have you ever felt like God was not likely to bless you on a given day because you missed your quiet time? That's legalism. Holiness by performance. But legalism never liberates. Only the gospel of grace liberates. Only the Spirit can truly set us free. But precisely how does this work? Let's take a sin we all obviously struggle with: lust.

> Legalism never liberates. Only the gospel of grace liberates.

In a sex-saturated society, is it really possible for us to conquer the sin of lust in our lives? God's Word teaches us that we can. We have already seen this in Romans 6: "we too may live a new life" (v. 4); "set free from sin" (v. 7); "sin shall no longer be your master" (v. 14); "you have been set free from sin" (v. 18). And that same chapter, coupled with the two ensuing chapters, shows us how. It all relates to how the Holy Spirit applies Christ's death and resurrection in our lives. In this fundamental dimension of human life, our sexuality, we can truly enjoy the freedom of God's holiness! Let's do a case study.

Suppose, men, you're walking along one beautiful spring day, enjoying your life as a Christian, when a vision of loveliness crosses your path and you're immediately tempted to lust. Well, first of all, don't beat yourself up for being tempted. It is not a sin to be tempted. God never promised us a struggle-free Christian life. There will always be an internecine warfare in our lives between our sinful nature and the Holy Spirit: "They are in conflict with each other, so that you are not to do whatever you want" (Gal. 5:17). So there will always be the possibility of temptation. But Jesus himself was "tempted in every way, just as we are—yet he did not sin" (Heb. 4:15). "Because he himself suffered when he was tempted, he is able to help those who are being tempted" (Heb. 2:18)—that's us! But back to our case study. How do we get the help we need? As is true with about everything in our Christian walk, our help comes through prayer.

I still have a vivid memory of a somewhat embarrassing conversation I had with two of my seminary friends in the dorm one day. As single young men, we all struggled with lust, and we were discussing just precisely how we should deal with it. I grew increasingly uncomfortable and decided to quote Billy Graham and hopefully end this uncomfortable discussion. I said, "Billy Graham says to avoid the second look." There, that's the definitive answer, so let's move on. But then one of my friends added, "My problem is that I don't take my eyes off of them the first time." We finally gave up on finding the ultimate answer.

Later, however, I came across a statement by the great Presbyterian preacher, Lloyd John Olgivie, which addressed this very issue. It relates to what Paul says about having the mindset (*phronema*) of the Spirit instead of the mindset of the flesh (Rom. 8:5–8). The crucial decision lies with whether we set our minds on what the flesh desires or on what the Spirit desires. When we are tempted to have the mindset of the flesh ("she's a beautiful woman whom I would use for my own selfish desires"), we simply choose to pray for the young lady ("Lord, thank you for her beauty; bless her in every way"). Now she's a person instead of an object. Through prayer, we've tapped into the power of the Spirit and we're able to enjoy her beauty while at the same time seeing her as a person—someone's daughter, someone's sister, someone's present or future spouse. It's like trying to keep the image of a pink elephant from entering your mind: You can't, unless you deliberately turn your attention to something else. In prayer, we can turn our attention to God and receive the help of his Spirit to see a beautiful woman as a *person* made in God's image.

The same principle of dependent prayer applies in every arena of life. We need to learn afresh what it means to pray in the Spirit, to live in the Spirit, to be continually filled with the Spirit. In short, the church at present is lacking in a theology of Christian *growth*. It should be as important to us as the new birth or spiritual empowerment for bold witness, even with signs and wonders. After all, our testimonies and spiritual gifts sound hollow without accompanying love, joy, peace, patience, kindness, goodness, faithfulness, gentleness, and self-control—in short, godly, Christlike character.

CHAPTER SIX
GOD'S PENTECOSTAL WORK

This chapter would probably not have been included in this volume had it not been for the greatest revival movement in the history of Christianity. Before January 1, 1901, there was no such thing as a "Pentecostal" Christian. Today there are more than six hundred million of them! And the movement continues to expand, especially among the developing nations of Asia, Africa, and Latin America. In America alone, between 1901 and 1932, more than two hundred new Pentecostal denominations were formed. Today, denominations such as the Assemblies of God and the Church of God lead the way in church growth in America, while many other evangelical and mainline denominations continue to decline. It may be true that the Pentecostals' most important contribution is that of spiritual vitality. But it is also becoming increasingly clear that they have a theological contribution to make as well.

Some of the leading systematic theologians and biblical scholars in the world today claim a Pentecostal or charismatic heritage. They have helped us to understand, for example, that Luke was more than a historian. He had a theological contribution to make as well. One of the first volumes to point this out was the little classic by Roger Stronstad, *The Charismatic Theology of St. Luke.*[1] In the foreword of this volume, theologian Clark Pinnock wrote: "Watch out you evangelicals—the

---

1 (Peabody, Mass.: Hendrickson, 1984).

young Pentecostal scholars are coming!"[2] Too often evangelicals—and that includes all of us who believe in the authority of the Bible and the primacy of evangelism—haven't given full attention to Luke's strong emphasis on the charismatic dimension of the Holy Spirit's work. Luke uses the Spirit baptism metaphor to point to the empowerment of the church for her end time ministry. So when a Pentecostal asks you, "Have you received the baptism, brother?" they want to know whether you've been *empowered* by the Spirit. It was easier for me to be open to their message because of Aunt Lou and Uncle Wilbur.

> Luke uses the Spirit baptism metaphor to point to the empowerment of the church for her end time ministry.

These sterling Pentecostal saints exuded the love and joy of the Lord. And they were bold in prayer and witness. Miracles were almost commonplace in their lives and in their church. When I visited their Pentecostal church in Carlsbad, New Mexico, I was a little frightened, as a young Southern Baptist boy, by the exuberance of their worship, but also attracted to the powerful sense of the presence of God in their midst. I decided I wanted whatever it was they had. What they had was the Holy Spirit. Later I would discover that I too had the Spirit, but had never fully tapped into the charismatic, empowering dimension of his work in my life. Having been an active participant in the renewal for going on five decades now, I can testify that our dear Pentecostal brothers and sisters have awakened us to the Spirit's empowering work in unparalleled fashion and we owe them a tremendous debt. They get their name from one of the key events in redemptive history: Pentecost.

When I began doing research for the chapter on salvation and the work of the Spirit in my own systematic theology text, I made a major discovery.

---

2 Stronstad, *The Charismatic Theology of St. Luke*, vii.

Systematic theology as a whole at that time simply ignored this event. Only Luke gives us the account of this astounding event which launched the church on her worldwide mission. Pentecost, then, was more than a historical event. It was an experience of empowerment still available to the church today. Southern Baptist leader, Ken Hemphill, has stated it well:

Pentecost marks the beginning and the empowering of the New Testament church. It marks a unique transformation in the lives of the members of the early church. After Pentecost we see high-voltage Christianity. If we ourselves and our churches do not have a Pentecost experience, we will never be bold witnesses and never know supernatural church growth.[3]

I have served for many years on the faculty of a university that embraced 3D Christianity from its inception. Here is how its founder, Oral Roberts, expressed the vision of the university to its founding class:

Your spiritual development includes a new birth through repentance and faith in the Lord Jesus Christ, a constant cleansing of your inner self from sin, the baptism in the Holy Spirit in the charismatic dimension for empowerment and personal edification, a manifestation of the gifts of the Holy Spirit through you for meeting the needs of others, a personal witness of your Master to your fellow man, and a daily application of Christian principles to the demands of daily life.[4]

So, in effect, in this chapter we will be exploring this "baptism in the Holy Spirit in the charismatic dimension for empowerment and personal

3   Ken Hemphill, *The Antioch Effect* (Nashville: Broadman & Holman, 1994), pp. 27-28.
4   *Oral Roberts University Catalogue*, Volume 21, No. 1, 2000-2002, Oral Roberts University, Tulsa, Oklahoma, 15.

edification." Some may be immediately put off by this language. In good Pauline fashion they would assert, "I've already been baptized in the Holy Spirit. First Corinthians 12:13 states: 'In one Spirit we were all baptized into one body' (ESV)." And they would be correct. Paul clearly uses the Spirit baptism metaphor in the initiatory sense in this passage. But Luke uses the same metaphor to point to the empowering dimension of the work of the Spirit, and we desperately need to give him a full hearing in our day! In other words, Jesus' end time work of baptizing in the Spirit encompasses all three dimensions: new birth, sanctification, and empowerment.

> Jesus' end time work of baptizing in the Spirit encompasses all three dimensions: new birth, sanctification, and empowerment.

Luke's two-part history—Luke-Acts—is riveting. Luke's *theology* is enriching as well! His is a "salvation history." Perhaps the theme verse for his entire work, which comprises some twenty-seven percent of the New Testament, would be Jesus' own words, "For the Son of Man came to seek and to save the lost" (Luke 19:10).[5] Luke, a Gentile, wants us to appreciate the salvation that God is offering to all of humanity, Jew and Gentile. And Luke highlights certain elements of society: women, children, the poor, and social outcasts. He vividly portrays Jesus' liberating ministry on their behalf. People are always praying and praising God in Luke. He strongly accents the Spirit's charismatic activities. It is an exciting read![6]

What is the key to the world-changing ministry of Jesus and the early church? Without question, Luke tells us, it is the power of the Holy Spirit. And precisely how do we tap into this power? Again, Luke's answer is

---

5   A pioneering work in this field of study is I. Howard Marshall's classic, *Luke: Historian and Theologian* (Grand Rapids: Zondervan, 1971).

6   I encourage the reader to read straight through Luke-Acts in *The Books of the Bible*, NIV (Grand Rapids: Zondervan), which presents the plain text without verses and chapters. It reads like an engaging modern-day novel.

clear: prayer. Without question, Luke links prayer and the power of the Spirit. And his narrative is laced with stories that illustrate this dynamic. We'll begin with the infancy narratives of the first two chapters of Luke.

It was a once in a lifetime opportunity. Zechariah had been chosen by lot to offer incense to the Lord in the sanctuary. Luke makes a comment that is easy to miss. He says "all the assembled worshipers were praying outside" (Luke 1:10). Anytime something momentous is about to happen in Luke's story, it is accompanied by prayer. In this case, Gabriel was about to announce to Zechariah that he and his wife were going to have a baby! Elizabeth was not able to conceive and now both husband and wife were very old. They had evidently prayed many long years for a child. The angel said, "Do not be afraid, Zechariah; your prayer has been heard. Your wife Elizabeth will bear you a son, and you are to call him John" (v. 13). But this will be no ordinary child "for he will be great in the sight of the Lord" and "he will be filled with the Holy Spirit even before he is born" (v. 15). John the Baptist would be the forerunner of the Messiah himself. Since the prophetic voice had been silent for four hundred years, John's ministry would create quite a stir. In fact, many thought he himself might be the Messiah. He had quite a following. In fact, some thirty-five years after Pentecost, Paul would encounter some disciples of John the Baptist at Ephesus (Acts 19:1–7). But prayer was the key to the whole event—the prayers of the people outside the temple and certainly the prayers of Zechariah and Elizabeth. Note also the astounding announcement that John would be filled with the Holy Spirit in his mother's womb!

Later, Mary and Joseph would return to the temple to present Jesus, and more astonishing things would happen. There was an old woman there named Anna, who came to Mary and Joseph. "She never left the temple but worshiped night and day, fasting and praying," Luke tells us (v. 38). Anna "gave thanks to God and spoke about the child to all who were looking forward to the redemption of Jerusalem" (v. 38). Only Luke relates these stories, and prayer sets the atmosphere for all these marvelous events. Earlier that day at the Temple, Simeon, a "righteous and devout" man would have a similar prophetic word for Mary and Joseph: "the Holy Spirit was on him. It had been revealed to him by the Holy Spirit that he would not die before he had seen the Lord's Messiah. Moved by the Spirit, he went into the temple courts" (vv. 25–27). Simeon gave a beautiful prophetic word concerning Jesus. Notice in all this—prayer and the Spirit!

The time comes for Jesus to launch his earthly ministry. Jesus goes to John the Baptist to be baptized by him. Luke's account of this momentous event is much briefer than those of Matthew, Mark, and John. And he adds a unique historical detail not mentioned in the other accounts.

> When all the people were being baptized, Jesus was baptized too. And as he was praying, heaven was opened and the Holy Spirit descended on him in bodily form like a dove. And a voice came from heaven: "You are my Son, whom I love; with you I am well pleased" (vv. 21–22).

Notice only Luke tells us that it was *while Jesus was praying* that the Spirit descended and the Father spoke, empowering and endorsing Jesus' messianic ministry. Prayer and the power of the Spirit!

Well, Jesus' ministry takes off, and the crowds multiply. Today, if this happened to us, we would set up a book table and take all their names and addresses for our mailing list. But Jesus did just the opposite. Everyone wanted to hear him and be healed by him. "But Jesus often withdrew to lonely places and prayed" (Luke 5:16). Jesus spent the whole night in prayer before he chose the twelve apostles, and, again, only Luke tells us this (Luke 6:12–16). Only Luke tells us that it was *while Jesus was praying* that Peter had his great revelation at Caesarea Philippi (Luke 9:18–20). And, again, only Luke mentions that it was while Jesus was praying that he was transfigured (v. 29). We find parallel accounts of all these events in the other three gospels, but none of them mentions prayer. Luke is relating historical fact for spiritual purpose. He wants us to notice that Jesus' powerful ministry was so because of prayer.

We had voluntary chapels in the seminary I attended as a student. I loved to hear the majestic anthems of the choirs! But one day they sang a simple little song that has haunted me the rest of my life. The song asked, "If Jesus needed to pray, how about you?" If Jesus, the sinless Son of God, in perfect harmony with the Father, felt the need to pray, how much more should we? When David Yonggi Cho is asked how they built the world's largest church in Seoul, Korea, he always responds, "We pray and we obey." And then he laughs. We pragmatic Americans want techniques and strategies. We make our elaborate plans and *then* pray and ask God to bless them. The lesson of Pentecost is that prayer comes first. We tap into the Pentecostal dimension of the Holy Spirit's work through prayer. Prayer is primary. Jesus explicitly taught this truth.

> We tap into the Pentecostal dimension of the Holy Spirit's work through prayer. Prayer is primary. Jesus explicitly taught this truth.

"One day Jesus was praying in a certain place," Luke tells us, and one of Jesus' disciples said, "Lord, teach us to pray, just as John taught his disciples" (Luke 11:1). Today, we have allowed too many other *good* things to crowd out prayer. We would be more likely to ask Jesus today, "Lord, teach us to preach the way John Hagee preaches" or "Lord, teach us to teach the way Joyce Meyers teaches" or "Lord, teach us to heal the way Benny Hinn heals" or "Lord, teach us to lead the way John Maxwell leads." But this disciple had walked with Jesus and observed him long enough to know the secret to Jesus' ministry. Lord, teach us to pray! And so he does.

First, he gives us a wonderful pattern for prayer (vv. 2–4). We call it the Lord's Prayer but it is really the disciples' prayer. Next he tells an endearing story (parable) which teaches praying with persistence or "shameless audacity" (vv. 5–8). Then he gives his famous Ask, Seek, and Knock teaching that we usually associate with the Sermon on the Mount. But in this context he adds a little twist. In the Sermon on the Mount, Jesus says that if we who are evil know how to give good gifts to our children, how much more will our Father in heaven give *good things* to those who ask him (Matt. 7:11). Here in Luke, Jesus says, "how much more will your Father in heaven give the Holy Spirit to those who ask him!" (Luke 11:13).

Using again a characteristic method of teaching, a parable, Jesus reminds earthly fathers that they would never give a snake for a fish or a scorpion for an egg. *How much more then*, can we count on our heavenly Father! "If you then, though you are evil, know how to give good gifts to your children, how much more will your Father in heaven give the Holy Spirit to those who ask him!" God's greatest gift is the gift of his Spirit. Remember, Jesus is still teaching on prayer. We receive the greatest help in our prayers from the Holy Spirit. Paul describes this help in these terms: "In the same way, the Spirit helps us in our weakness. We do not know what we ought to pray for, but the Spirit himself intercedes for us through wordless groans. And he who searches our hearts knows the mind of the Spirit, because the Spirit intercedes for God's people in accordance with the will of God" (Rom. 8:26–27). Again, 3D Christianity—help in our prayers provided by our Triune God!

Also, remember that earlier in this teaching on prayer, Jesus taught us to pray for "daily bread" (v. 3). Life is so daily. We need the daily supply of the Spirit's power to be the prayerful, obedient disciples Jesus desires. We need to be *continually* filled with the Holy Spirit (Eph. 5:18).[7] I'm a little weary (if not wary) of testimonies to being "Spirit-filled" as if this were a one-time event. I'm glad to hear how God dramatically invaded your life two decades ago. But what about today? Is your walk consistent? Is your prayer life up-to-date? How fruitful is your walk at present? When was the last time you shared your faith? Do you live a life of humble service to those around you? This is the kind of prayer life and lifestyle Jesus is teaching here.

Jesus used other parables to teach us the lifestyle of prayer in the Holy Spirit. In Luke 18 we find two very interesting stories: one about a persistent widow and an unjust judge (vv. 1–8) and another about a self-righteous Pharisee and a repentant tax collector (vv. 9–14). Luke prefaces the stories with these words: "Then Jesus told his disciples a parable to show them that they should always pray and not give up" (v. 1). We need this encouragement! How easy it is to become discouraged and give up in our prayers. We're living in the end times. They started with Jesus. And these two stories are prefaced with a teaching by Jesus on the coming of the kingdom (Luke 17:20–37). In this present evil age there will always be tribulations. Life is filled with struggles and challenges. And prayer is our most precious resource. God will come through for his people; and if you take a peek in the back of the book, you'll find that *we win*! So we should be like the persistent widow and never give up. She is like our spiritual Winston Churchill! From the Pharisee and tax collector, we should learn to avoid self-righteousness like the plague and to be quick to repent.

As we move toward the end of Luke's gospel, we find Jesus entering into the tribulations of the passion week—with prayer. He is also preparing his disciples for their coming trials. And his number one word

---

7 I am indebted for these insights to George T. Montague, *The Holy Spirit: The Growth of a Biblical Tradition* (New York: Paulist Press, 1976), 258-260.

of advice is, Pray! "Jesus went out as usual to the Mount of Olives, and his disciples followed him" (Luke 22:39). Twice he tells them to pray that they will not fall into temptation (vv. 40, 46). The word for temptation here is *peirasmos*, which can be variously translated trial, temptation, calamity, or affliction. Remember Jesus' pattern for prayer, which ended with, "And lead us not into temptation [*peirasmos*]": Lead us not into hard testing, temptation, the time of trial! And now Jesus sets the example.

The prayer that follows is one of the most important recorded prayers in the Scriptures. We should observe it carefully and learn from it.

> He withdrew about a stone's throw beyond them, knelt down and prayed, "Father, if you are willing, take this cup from me; yet not my will, but yours be done." An angel from heaven appeared to him and strengthened him. And being in anguish, he prayed more earnestly and his sweat was like drops of blood falling to the ground (Luke 22:41–44).

First, Jesus withdrew from others and knelt down. When was the last time you did that? There will be times in life when it is a necessity, but it should also be a pattern in life. Humble submission. A cry for help. Jesus expresses a desire to be exempted from the coming suffering, yet also prays, "not my will but yours be done" (v. 42).

Prayer is not about getting God to do our will. Prayer is about asking God to help us to embrace *his* will. The struggle of prayer is not in getting God to change, but in getting ourselves to change. I have noticed that God never takes my advice. He doesn't need it. Prayer positions us for *God's* will—his better plans, his better purposes. This is graduate level faith. Learning to trust God when we don't understand, when life doesn't make sense, when suffering abounds with no relief in sight. Jesus was in anguish that day. He was facing unspeakable suffering. And yet he submitted to the Father's purposes in those sufferings. Something else happens, something wonderful: "An angel from heaven appeared to him and strengthened him" (v. 43).

Prayer brings comfort, encouragement, and strength—sometimes administered by the angels themselves! When God's people pray, things stir in the heavenly realms. If God opened our eyes to it, we would be shocked. Prayer is not self-help mantras, psyching ourselves to feel better. It is interaction with God Almighty.

> Prayer is not about getting God to do our will. Prayer is about asking God to help us to embrace *his* will.

Jesus would drink the cup of suffering. And even as the soldiers were driving the cruel spikes through Jesus' hands and feet, *he is praying—for them!* And for all of us, really: "Father, forgive them, for they do not know what they are doing" (Luke 23:34). Only Luke, among the gospel writers, records this prayer. It is astounding. With Jesus' own words we already begin to see the significance of his cross: Forgiveness. And one of the criminals would grasp it: "Jesus, remember me when you come into your kingdom" (v. 42). What an incredible act of faith! Jesus responded, "Truly I tell you, today you will be with me in paradise" (v. 43).

Once I was invited to preach at a Unitarian church. The pastor warned me that if I stepped into the pulpit and opened a Bible, that I would alienate half of the congregation. I responded that the Bible was all I did preach. I didn't preach *Psychology Today* or *Newsweek*. He gave me full liberty to preach whatever I chose. I chose to preach this story about the thief on the cross and was amazed at the response. This story was one of the most powerful events in the entire passion narrative. A suffering, dying, *praying* Jesus! His final words would be a prayer: "Father, into your hands I commit my spirit" (v. 46). Luke even tells us the attending centurion was powerfully impacted by the manner in which Jesus died (v. 47). And so should we be.

But did the disciples pick up on Jesus' pattern of prayer? He made sure that they would. He prepared them for the empowering of the Spirit. It was Easter Sunday night, Luke tells us, when Jesus appeared to them, showed them the marks of his passion, ate some fish in their presence, then revealed to them the saving significance of his life and ministry as foretold throughout the Hebrew Scriptures (Luke 24:36–47). If the disciples had been Southern Baptists (my mother church, which I love), they would have responded, "That's it. We're ready to go. We've seen the risen Lord and we've got the Bible stuff down pat. Let's get our committees up and running and save this rotten world." But Jesus said to wait; they weren't ready yet: "Stay in the city until you have been clothed with power from on high" (v. 49).

"Do not leave Jerusalem," Jesus explained, "but wait for the gift my Father promised, which you have heard me speak about. For John baptized with water, but in a few days you will be baptized with the Holy Spirit" (Acts 1:4–5). Then he added, "You will receive power when the Holy Spirit comes on you; and you will be my witnesses in Jerusalem, in all Judea and Samaria, and to the ends of the earth" (v. 8). So what did the disciples do? "They all joined together in prayer, along with the women and Mary the mother of Jesus, and with his brothers" (v. 14). Prayer—then Pentecost, where they were all "filled with the Holy Spirit and began to speak in other tongues as the Spirit enabled them" (Acts 2:4). After Peter's message "about three thousand were added to their number" (v. 41), and they did four things: "They devoted themselves to the apostles' teaching and to fellowship, to the breaking of bread and to prayer" (v. 42). If the twenty-first-century churches would do those four things, we would have healthy, vital churches. Perhaps prayer is the most neglected.

Next, Peter and John get called before the religious authorities for their preaching and healing ministry. And upon their release, they go to their friends *for a prayer meeting*, asking God for continued boldness and healings, signs, and wonders. The results of the prayer meeting were immediate and dramatic: "After they had prayed, the place where they were meeting was shaken. And they were all filled with the Holy Spirit and spoke the word of God boldly" (Acts 4:31). It was like a little Pentecost! Later, the apostles instruct the growing congregation to select seven men to take care of practical ministries so that the apostles can fully devote themselves "to prayer and the ministry of the word" (Acts 6:4). After the gospel spread into Samaria, Peter and John were sent from Jerusalem by the other apostles to Samaria. "When they arrived, they prayed for the new believers there that they might receive the Holy Spirit" (Acts 8:15).

After Jesus arrests Saul on the road to Damascus, he commissions Ananias to pray for Saul, informing Ananias that "at this moment he is praying, and he has seen in a vision a man named Ananias come in and lay his hands on him so that he might regain his sight" (Acts 9:11–12 NRSV). When Ananias lays his hands on Saul, he tells him that Jesus has sent Ananias "so that you may see again and be filled with the Holy Spirit" (v. 17). Saul spends some time with the disciples at Damascus, then Luke adds: "At once he began to preach in the synagogues that Jesus is the Son of God" (v. 20). Prayer, infilling of the Spirit, bold preaching—sounds like a good formula for the present-day church!

The breakthrough of the gospel among the Gentiles is equally dramatic. At Caesarea, there was a devout Roman centurion, who "gave generously to those in need and prayed to God regularly" (Acts 10:2), About three, one afternoon, Cornelius has a vision of an angel. The angel says, "Your prayers and gifts to the poor have come up as a memorial offering before God" (v. 4). He is instructed to send messengers to Peter. "About noon the following day as they were on their journey and approaching the city, Peter went up on the roof to pray" (v. 9), and he has a dramatic vision preparing him to open up to the Gentiles as candidates for the gospel. Later at Cornelius's house, Cornelius explains to Peter: "About three days ago I was in my house praying at this hour, at three in the afternoon. Suddenly a man in shining clothes stood before me and said, 'Cornelius, God has heard your prayer and remembered your gifts to the poor'" (vv. 30–31). Later, the church's fervent prayers for Peter resulted in his miraculous deliverance from prison (Acts 12:5, 12). Prayer, prayer, prayer! Luke makes sure that we don't miss the picture. Prayer brings the mighty power of God for the spread of the gospel.

We may never agree on precisely what to call this empowerment—baptism in the Spirit, infilling of the Spirit, or perhaps we could agree to call it in contemporary terms simply "getting zapped by God"—but we definitely need it. We may not agree on the doctrinal nomenclature, but surely we can agree on the necessity of prayer. Anyone who has ever attended a Billy Graham crusade can testify to the power of prayer.

I attended one of Dr. Graham's last crusades in Louisville, Kentucky at Papa John Stadium. It was the first night of the crusade. Dr. Graham was weak in body. He sat to preach and spoke for only about fifteen minutes. Then came the invitation. The field was covered with people walking forward in response to the gospel invitation. During a pause Graham said that this was an unusually large response for the first night of a crusade and that he believed it was because of all the prayers that had preceded the meetings. For an entire year, Christians from every background are praying and preparing for the meetings. The atmosphere in the meetings is electric. Unity in prayer brings power!

Prayer is multi-dimensional, moving heaven and earth. It is the most powerful force on earth. The Pentecostal dimension of the work of the Holy Spirit empowers our witness and ministry. Sharing our faith becomes a natural—and supernatural!—overflow of the Spirit's presence in our lives, rather than a "sales pitch." Prayer flows continually as the heart cry to God. Prayer in the Spirit becomes as natural as breathing. Our service to others becomes an expression of spiritual giftedness. Gifts such as words of wisdom, words of knowledge, faith, healings, miracles, prophecies, discerning of spirits, tongues, interpretation of tongues, serving, teaching, encouraging, giving, leading, and showing mercy enhance the ministry of the church.

As a seminary professor, one of my responsibilities is overseeing applied research projects for some of our Doctor of Ministry students. James Simmons, a Southern Baptist pastor of a very traditional congregation in Murray, Kentucky, felt strongly led to reestablish an ongoing discipleship program in his church as a part of his Doctor of Ministry work. One aspect of the training program was an exploration of the spiritual gifts mentioned in the New Testament with a view toward enabling his parishioners to discover what areas of service God might have in mind for them. No charism mentioned was left out, including the more controversial ones such as healing and tongues. What surprised both the pastor and his people was the amazing discovery of how many spiritual gifts were already in operation in their midst, including faith and authority over the demonic. Very often all that is needed in a given congregation is simply enabling the members to become aware of what the Holy Spirit is already doing in their midst![8]

3D Christianity, then, has these three dimensions of the work of the Holy Spirit: paschal, purifying, and Pentecostal. It involves conversion, consecration, and charisma. It is the kind of Christianity we see displayed in the Book of Acts. It is a revolutionary Christianity, a world-changing Christianity. We enter into life's greatest adventure—being co-laborers

---

8   James L. Simmons, "Renewing a Discipleship Program at the Memorial Baptist Church," Unpublished D.Min. Applied Research Project Report, School of Theology and Missions, Oral Roberts University, Tulsa, Oklahoma, May 2002.

with God with a purpose in life that serves both time and eternity. The Holy Spirit himself directs and empowers our mission. Ben Witherington's study of Acts corroborates this conclusion and states quite aptly: "The Holy Spirit, then, is the means, the person who empowers the disciples as well as Jesus for preaching, teaching, and healing."[9] His comment forms a natural segue to our next section, which explores more in-depth how God works through us.

---

9 Ben Witherington III, *The Acts of the Apostles: A Socio-Rhetorical Commentary* (Grand Rapids: Eerdmans, 1998), 70.

HOW
GOD
WORKS
THROUGH US

CHAPTER SEVEN
TEACHING

Controversy always seemed to swirl around Jesus. Generally, the common folk heard him gladly. But the religious leaders, with their vested interest in staying in authority (notice they were always asking him about who gave him his authority), developed a deadly resolve to summarily remove Jesus. One day, the division and conflict was so intense that they sent the police, the temple guard, to arrest him (John 7:32). It was the Pharisees, the authorized teachers of the Law, and the chief priests who had hatched the plot on this occasion, which was the Festival of Tabernacles. But the temple police returned empty-handed. When asked why, they simply replied, "No one ever spoke the way this man does" (v. 45). This response predictably provoked the ire of the religious leaders.

But why did those temple guards not bring Jesus in as they had been ordered to do? It would have been a simple thing to arrest Jesus. No one would have been able to stop them. It was because they began to listen to what Jesus was saying. Jesus' teaching was mesmerizing. From the very beginning it was so: "The people were amazed at his teaching, because he taught them as one who had authority, not as their teachers of the law" (Mark 1:22). It was who Jesus was, what he was saying, and how he was saying it that stopped the guards in their tracks.

Jesus was a great teacher. He called himself a teacher. Others called him a teacher. He was often addressed as Rabbi, Master. He didn't have the formal training of the religious leaders, but he taught in their synagogues, reasoned with them, and developed his own band of disciples. But he was different in other ways as well. He taught out among the people in the open air and welcomed people his religious opponents shunned—women, children, and sinners of all stripes. He conversed with these people, ate with them, welcomed them.[1] Jesus claimed a role in a venerable tradition. The *Torah* itself, in a broader sense, meant "instruction." Moses was called to teach (Deut. 4:14), as were the Levites (Lev. 10:11; Deut. 33:10).[2] The rabbis of Jesus' day followed in that teaching tradition. And Jesus had the audacity, the *chutzpah*, to insert himself into the conversation!

Matthew's gospel accents Jesus' teaching role, coupling five great teachings of Jesus with a related narrative section. Before the first two of them, the Sermon on the Mount (Matt. 5:1–7:29) and the Mission Discourse (Matt. 9:35–10:42), Matthew provides a programmatic summary of Jesus' ministry. In both instances Jesus is described as (1) teaching in their synagogues, (2) preaching the good news of the kingdom, and (3) healing every disease and sickness (Matt. 4:23; 9:35). As the Body of Christ, shouldn't we expect to continue that ministry? "Jesus Christ is the same yesterday and today and forever" (Heb. 13:8). 3D Christianity, then, will be fully functional in all three dimensions of kingdom work. First, we must look at Jesus' ministry, and then we must follow through to discover how he wants to work through us today.

Jesus, as a communicator, was never boring. He refused to drone on, citing one rabbi after another, in paralyzing prose that put his hearers to sleep. His language and images were fresh, drawn from nature and everyday life. He was colorful, unpredictable, sometimes humorous. He utilized proverbs, metaphors, similes, puns, riddles, paradox, hyperbole, and irony. He always kept you a little off balance and forced you to think. He is simply the most delightful and disturbing teacher you will

---

1 See Robert H. Stein, *Jesus the Messiah: A Survey of the Life of Christ* (Downers Grove, Ill.: InterVarsity Press, 1996), 123.

2 Everett F. Harrison, *A Short Life of Christ* (Grand Rapids: Eerdmans, 1968), 94–95.

ever hear. No one has matched him in the history of civilization, nor will they ever. The uniqueness of Jesus' teaching alone is positive proof that we are dealing here with someone who is more than a man. He is God's one and only Son.

Today, Jesus the teacher is infinitely more popular in general culture than his followers. Historian John Dickson discovered this after being interviewed about Jesus on a secular radio station. When the phone lines were opened for callers to respond, their opinions were quite surprising:

> To my surprise, while most callers had negative things to say about Christians or the church, every caller heaped praise on Jesus himself. They loved his ethics, his example, his critique of religion and his general approach to life and faith. In their view, he was the ultimate guru-figure, a teacher among teachers. It is probably fair to say that Jesus' teaching is the most famous aspect of his ministry. We don't know what to make of his healings or his death and resurrection, but his *words* still resonate all these years later. Some have become proverbial in the English language: "the blind leading the blind," "turn the other cheek," "salt of the earth," "seek and you will find" and many others.[3]

Jesus loved to make statements and tell stories that made people stop and ponder. He seldom spelled it out for them. Riddles and parables were common in his speech. He could even take a well-known scripture and turn it into a riddle.

One of the best-known messianic passages of his time was Psalm 110:1. On Tuesday of Passion Week, Jesus' fielded the challenges and questions of the religious leaders and then had a question of his own:

---

3   John Dickson, *Life of Jesus: Who He Is and Why He Matters* (Grand Rapids: Zondervan, 2010), 73.

Then Jesus said to them, "Why is it said that the Messiah is the son of David? David himself declares in the Book of Psalms: 'the Lord said to my Lord: "Sit at my right hand until I make your enemies a footstool for your feet."' David calls him 'Lord.' How then can he be his son?" (Luke 20:41–44).

Basically, Jesus was confronting them with David's prophetic words and raising the question, "Who was David's Lord here?" He wanted them to discover that the one superior to David was Jesus himself! Probably, most of them didn't "get it" till later.

Every time I read this story, I think of a riddle I've told all my life. I usually test my classes with it before I turn to this passage: A man was going to be hanged the next morning. He was told that if he could come up with a riddle that no one could answer, he would be spared. On the gallows the next morning, he spoke these words: "Brothers and sisters have I none, but that man's father (and he points to someone standing in front) is my father's son. What is our relationship?" Usually there's a long pause, then someone will blurt out, "It's his uncle!" "No," I respond, "he would have had to say, 'That man's father is my father's *brother.*'" Then someone says, "It's his brother!" But I point out that he says he has no brothers. So what's the answer to this riddle? Spoiler alert! If you're wanting to wrestle with this a little longer, don't read any further. Are you ready? The man on the gallows is pointing to his son!

In the same way, Jesus wanted his opponents to make the discovery that Jesus is Yahweh, David's Lord, the Messiah! He would, of course, be lynched for blasphemy later for making this claim. Notice here though, that Jesus is *subtle*. He only raises the question. By the end of the week, all the evidence of Jesus' public words and deeds would point to messianic claims, even claims to divinity. And the religious leaders were simply not willing to countenance that possibility. They would condemn Jesus to a Roman crucifixion.

Here's another of Jesus' famous riddles: "Destroy this temple, and I will raise it again in three days" (John 2:19). He was referring, of course, to his physical body rather than the temple where they worshiped. These words would later be thrown back into Jesus' face (Matt. 26:61; Mark 14:58; Matt. 27:40; Mark 15:29). His opponents never got it! Or how about this one: "How can Satan drive out Satan? If a kingdom is divided against itself, that kingdom cannot stand" (Mark 3:23–24). The teachers of the law had attributed Jesus' powers to the devil (v. 22), and Jesus' question stopped them in their tracks. And Jesus used other figures of speech as well.

In describing our mission as his disciples, Jesus used a number of literary devices:

> *Simile:* "Go! I am sending you out like lambs among wolves" (Luke 10:3).

> *Metaphor:* "You are the salt of the earth. . . . You are the light of the world" (Matt. 5:13, 14).

> *Paradox:* "For whoever wants to save their life will lose it, but whoever loses their life for me will save it" (Luke 9:24).

> *Hyperbole:* "If anyone comes to me and does not hate father and mother, wife and children, brothers and sisters—yes, even their own life—such a person cannot be my disciple" (Luke 14:26).[4]

But the one method of communicating that Jesus used as no one else did was the *parable*!

---

4 For a helpful chart of the common figures of speech used by Jesus, see: Mark L. Strauss, *Four Portraits, One Jesus: An Introduction to Jesus and the Gospels* (Grand Rapids: Zondervan, 2007), 437.

Jesus used these stories from everyday life to bring home a spiritual truth and he did it more often and more effectively than anyone. This was Jesus' best and best-known teaching device. Who hasn't heard the parables of the Good Samaritan (Luke 10:30–37) or the Prodigal Son (Luke 15:11–32)? But there are dozens of others. Stories are immediate attention-grabbers and they linger in our thoughts. And Jesus was the consummate storyteller. The overarching theme of the parables was the kingdom of God.

Jesus seemed obsessed with the kingdom of God. The kingdom is the rule or reign of God. We pray for God's kingdom to come, his will to be done, "on earth as it is in heaven" (Matt. 6:10). The parables illustrate the nature, power, and purpose of that kingdom. To embrace Christ is to embrace his kingdom. We embrace his command to love (Mark 12:29–31) and his commission to make disciples (Matt. 28:18–20). And notice that in the Great Commission, the imperative is given of "teaching them to obey everything I have commanded you" (v. 20).

Jesus' sermons were filled with sage advice as well. "For one thing he was known as a *teacher* in the tradition of the sages of Israel. Most of the tradition of Jesus' teaching falls under this heading."[5] And Jesus' own brother, James, was a wisdom teacher as well, giving us the quintessential wisdom book of the New Testament, the book of James, which strongly echoes Jesus' own teaching as well as other Jewish wisdom literature.[6] Teaching transforms. Perhaps teachers influence us more than anyone else. The wisdom we gain in the learning environment informs and influences everything we do. Jesus knew this, and the church has known it for more than twenty centuries. Even the business world

> Teaching transforms. Perhaps teachers influence us more than anyone else.

---

5 James D. G. Dunn, *Jesus, Paul, and the Gospels* (Grand Rapids: Eerdmans, 2011), 14 (Dunn's italics).
6 Dunn, *Jesus, Paul, and the Gospels,* 14.

has tuned in to this reality. David A. Garvin, C. Roland Christensen Professor of Business Administration at the Harvard Business School, recommends that businesses be learning organizations "skilled at creating, acquiring, and transferring knowledge, and at modifying its behavior to reflect new knowledge and insights."[7]

The church has always been a learning place. She spawned the whole university enterprise as well. And the leaders produced in our churches and schools have been effective in large measure because they were taught well. Albert Mohler argues: "The most effective leaders are unstoppable teachers. They teach by word, example, and sheer force of passion. They transform their corporations, institutions, and congregations into learning organizations. And the people they lead are active learners who add value and passion to the work."[8] Discipleship is about learning (teaching), sharing (preaching), and serving (healing). Unfortunately, we have too often forgotten that our commission is disciple-making (Matt. 28:18–20), and the teaching arm of the church has been allowed to atrophy in our day.

> So the Holy Spirit, sent from the Father, continues Jesus' teaching ministry in our lives—3D Christianity!

Being disciples and making disciples both entail teaching and learning. First and foremost, we *are* disciples—students, learners, followers—of Jesus. So Jesus' teaching ministry continues down to the present. But precisely how is this so? We recall Jesus words, "Anyone who loves me will obey my teaching" (John 14:23). Then he adds, "But the Advocate, the Holy Spirit, whom the Father will send in my name, will teach you all things and will remind you of everything I have said to you" (v. 26). So the Holy Spirit, sent from the Father, continues Jesus'

---

7   David A. Garvin, "Building a Learning Organization," *Harvard Business Review* 71, no.4 (July 1, 1993): 80; cited in Albert Mohler, *The Conviction to Lead* (Bloomington, Minn.: Bethany House, 2012), 68.

8   Mohler, *The Conviction to Lead*, 72–73.

teaching ministry in our lives—3D Christianity! The Holy Spirit gave us the Scriptures, which provide Jesus' teachings in written form. He also speaks to us directly. As the Reformers taught, the Spirit and the Scriptures work in tandem. The Spirit illumines the Scriptures and wields them as a sword (Eph. 6:17). We grieve him when we neglect the Scriptures, or when we ignore him while reading the Scriptures. I've seen it both ways, growing up in the church.

At times, I was given the impression that all we needed was correct interpretative methods and a mastery of the biblical data, implying that prayerful dependence on the Spirit's help was for the charismatic crowd. But then that same charismatic crowd too often twisted and tortured the Scriptures in the name of spiritual insight, or neglected careful examination of Scripture altogether. The Father intends to teach us and mature us and he is unrelenting in this quest.

So we are to *be* disciples, but we are also to *make* disciples, which we have already seen entails teaching them. When I think of disciple-making, I think of my old college roommate, Bill Hull. We played basketball together for Oral Roberts University. I had heard that we had recruited a hotshot Indiana basketball star. But the first time he walked out onto the court, I made two quick judgments, both of which proved to be false. With the sullen look on his face and all the beer-fat hanging off his body, Bill looked like a loss, both as a potential convert and as a basketball player. He quickly shed the fat and proved to be one of best players we've had at the university. Three weeks after his arrival, he met Christ. Later, he went with Oral Roberts on a crusade in Africa and was called to preach. And after graduation, he joined Athletes in Action of Campus Crusade for Christ as a player-coach for their basketball team.

It was with Crusade that Bill learned the importance of discipleship, a reality that had transformed his whole life. It was onward and upward from there. Now Bill is known internationally as a specialist in discipleship. He has published prolifically in this field (check Amazon!)

and travels the globe, giving seminars on the subject. He has pastored churches, planted churches, served as a top denominational leader, and preached globally. He is living proof that authentic discipleship is essential to the life of the church. And what was done for him, he continues to do for others on a one-on-one basis, making and mentoring new converts.

But what about teaching in the church today? We know that all of us should mature to the place that we can teach others (Heb. 5:12). We also know that some are gifted to teach (Rom. 12:7). At the same time, we are warned: "Not many of you should become teachers, my fellow believers, because you know that we who teach will be judged more strictly" (James 3:1). The teaching ministry of the church is serious business! We also need more pastor-teachers in our day.

Paul highlights the leadership of apostles, prophets, evangelists, pastors, and teachers in the church (Eph. 4:11), but the original language of the last two suggests that we may be looking at the idea of pastor-teachers here. We need more pastors who can teach. My family had wonderful pastors over the years, including many who were well-trained in the seminary. But the pastor who was the most helpful personally, my parents related to me, was one who had not had the privilege of professional training: On Wednesday nights in Bible studies, he would teach and then field their questions. If he knew the answer, he would share it. If he was unsure, he would say, "I'm not sure; let me study this a little more and get back with you." They learned more from him than from any other pastor because he got down on their level and was humbly sincere about helping them.

I think of Pastor Jack Hayford in our own day. I have had the privilege of teaching at his school a couple of times (once, team-teaching with him on the subject of homiletics and worship), and also attending services at the church. He is a tremendous leader of worship, who has also written some of the finest worship songs of our day. But he is also the quintessential pastor-teacher. If only more pastors in the Pentecostal/charismatic churches would follow his lead! Too often there is thin gruel indeed coming from our pulpits.

We have too many of what I call "text and tales preachers" today. They read a text and then tell a bunch of tales, many of which have little to do with the text. Some charismatic preachers I've heard have actually based the authority of their message more on what God supposedly said to them in their prayer closet than on the Bible itself. Many times prophecies are recorded and written down as if they were scriptures. There is too often greater enthusiasm for a "word from the Lord" than for the infallible Word of God. We need more expositional preaching and teaching, with pastors who are serious students of the Word, taking us on journeys through books of the Bible.

One of my favorite pastors is Dale Patterson of East Brent Baptist Church in Pensacola, Florida. Dale leads a powerful, praying church from a pulpit of rich expository preaching. This dynamite combination of Word and Spirit grew the church from four hundred to two thousand four hundred members. A church that is powerful in prayer and well-founded in the Scriptures will grow! I see the charismatic movement at a crisis point in this regard. Having largely lost the teaching ministry of the church, new generations of believers enter life biblically illiterate and bereft of doctrinal grounding. They are "infants, tossed back and forth by the waves, and blown here and there by every wind of teaching" (Eph. 4:14). Perhaps it's time for us to get back to Sunday school!

Yes, you read correctly—Sunday school! Done wrongly, Sunday school is deadly. I chafed at going to Sunday school during my junior high and high school years, since we spent more time discussing Friday night's football game or reading like first-graders from the quarterly. It wasn't until years later, attending seminary and pastoring my first church that I began to appreciate what Sunday school was actually designed to do. I discovered that every seven years that I was faithfully in Sunday school—and my parents made sure that I was!—that I had studied every verse of scripture from Genesis to Revelation. Couple that with solid biblical preaching from the pulpit and you have a well-founded believer!

When my seminary friend, Ken Hemphill, took the pastorate of First Baptist Church, Norfolk, Virginia, they had about four hundred members. He studied the history and purposes of Sunday school and decide to implement what he learned. The church grew to four thousand members. He discovered that virtually everything the church was supposed to be doing in terms of discipleship—evangelism, teaching, small groups, and spiritual oversight—could best be done through this one vehicle![9] It sounds shocking to say it, but perhaps one of the major ways we could revitalize dysfunctional charismatic churches, and there are many, would be to implement a substantive Sunday school program.

While completing my Ph.D. at the Southern Baptist Theological Seminary, I had the opportunity of planting a new church in the eastern end of Louisville, Kentucky. I got the idea from one of the professors at the seminary that Sunday school should be a "lay seminary." If we pastors needed seminary training for ministry, shouldn't those whom we are equipping for the work of the ministry (Eph. 4:12) need similar training? So we tried it in our new church. We offered Sunday school courses in church history, systematic theology, Christian ethics, and biblical Greek, along with various biblical and practical studies, and the people responded enthusiastically. And this was in a church that reveled in charismatic worship and prayer! It was a delightful integration of heart and head and we began to grow immediately both personally and numerically.

Jesus went about teaching. So should we. This ministry takes place both through our lips and our lives. It is indispensable to the ongoing life of the church. And it is a vital part of a 3D Christianity that teaches, preaches, and heals—like Jesus!

---

9   Ken Hemphill, *Revitalizing the Sunday Morning Dinosaur: A Sunday School Growth Strategy for the 21st Century* (Nashville: B & H, 1996).

CHAPTER EIGHT
PREACHING

Jesus was the greatest preacher who ever lived. We would expect to hear that said of Jesus out of deference to who he is. But it is factually true, precisely because of both who he was and what he had to say. He *is* the Word (John 1:1), the definitive revelation of God. And as the temple guards said, "No one ever spoke the way this man does" (John 7:46). Much of what has already been said about Jesus as a teacher in the previous chapter applies to his role as a preacher.

Jesus was a unique communicator. John Maxwell has often said that there is no excuse for a preacher to be boring. We preachers could learn from Jesus, because too often we are boring! But Jesus connected to his hearers even though what he had to say was often not pleasant to hear. For example, the first recorded word in his public proclamation was *repent*: "From that time on Jesus began to preach, 'Repent, for the kingdom of heaven has come near'" (Matt. 4:17). Repentance is not a popular message. Who wants to be told that they need to repent? Repent of what? Sin! And yet Jesus told us that the Holy Spirit would "prove the world to be in the wrong about sin and righteousness and judgment" (John 16:8). Those are not politically correct topics in our day, but in his day Jesus did not hesitate to address them. He confronted the sins of humanity and warned of a coming judgment. He preached more about hell, for example, than any preacher before or since. At the same time, he communicated the grace of God, both with his moving stories and his compassionate spirit.

We're all called to preach in one way or another. Not everyone is called to be a pastor or teacher, but everyone has a calling to a place of ministry in the body of Christ, which entails gospel ministry and building up the church (Eph. 4:12). We communicate Christ with our witness to his saving work and by our loving service in his name. But additionally there are those of us who have been called to a lifestyle of preaching and living by the gospel: "In the same way, the Lord has commanded that those who preach the gospel should receive their living from the gospel" (1 Cor. 9:14). And since I fit into that category, I would like to address for a moment the rest of us who have that calling upon their lives.

I believe that it was because my parents dedicated me to the Lord (by his sovereign and gracious promptings) that I have had a drive to know God all my life. Having met him at an early age, I thirsted for intimacy with him and was driven to his Word. I sensed his calling to preach early on, but did not share it with anyone. First of all, I couldn't relate to my ecclesial context in this regard. The preachers I observed often seemed a little strange to me. And the "preacher boys" in my church—those who had been called into "full-time Christian service" (I wondered why it was only boys and not girls)—were treated differently by everyone else. I simply couldn't fit into that mold and refused to mention the stirrings in my own life.

I recall sitting across from Oral Roberts at the lunch table in the cafeteria at ORU where I was a student, discussing this very issue. I said, "Brother Roberts, I simply can't relate to a lot of the seminary students on campus. They seem artificial, 'stained glass,' to me." He responded, "Larry, they're just trying to figure out who they are. It took me twelve years to discover who I was in the ministry." (He pastored twelve years before he went into healing evangelism.) As graduation approached, I knew that

I was going to have to deal with the calling to preach once and for all. It would affect all future decisions. I went into an empty dorm room and "had it out" with God. In those hours of prayer I came to the realization that God truly was calling me, that he wasn't going to withdraw that calling, and that the very best thing I could do was to surrender to that calling. I came out of that room with a clearer focus on who I was and what I was going to do with my life. Here are my humble comments to my fellow preachers on what it takes to be an effective preacher.

First, it takes a *conversion*. I'm serious! We have too many unregenerate clergy in our pulpits, This is one reason American Christianity is in a weakened state. We have preachers who have never been converted, and we have preachers who never preach for conversion. Oral Roberts always said, "You're only half through when you've finished the sermon." The other half is the call to decision. Billy Graham concurs. He has counseled numerous clergy over the years who have come to him in private, expressing no assurance of faith. He has often led them into a conversion experience. And who better calls people to conversion than Billy Graham! Leon Joseph Cardinal Suenens of Belgium, one of the four moderators of the Vatican II Council, was appointed by the pope to oversee Catholic charismatic renewal worldwide. Suenens later wrote that the message of the charismatic movement to the church is twofold: Be converted and be filled.[1]

Perhaps the charismatic renewal has done more to awaken us to these realities that any other movement. 3D Christianity is multi-dimensional, stressing regeneration, sanctification, and empowerment—all three. Suenens writes: "We must never forget that the Church cannot exist without its charismatic dimension; to be deprived of this dimension would not be merely an impoverishment, it would be a negation of the Church's very being."[2] As we have already seen, the Holy Spirit himself

---

1 See Leon Joseph Cardinal Suenens, *A New Pentecost?* (New York: Seabury, 1974).

2 Suenens, *A New Pentecost?* 8.

awakens us to these realities. He convicts of sin. He purifies our hearts. And he empowers and equips us for ministry.

Second, it takes a *calling* to make it as preachers. Sometimes it is that calling alone that will enable us to continue in gospel ministry. No one ever said it was going to be easy. It isn't. A young man is asleep upstairs on a Sunday morning. His mom calls from downstairs, "Son, get up and come down to breakfast. We're going to church." The young man responds, "I'm not going to church." There is silence for a while, and then his mom repeats, "Son, get up. We're going to church." And again the young man says, "I'm not going to church." So his mom marches upstairs, stands by his bed, and says, "Son, get up. We are going to church!" The son answers, "I'm not going to church for two reasons: They don't' like me and I don't like them." His mom replies, "Son, you are going to church for two reasons: You're forty years old and you're the pastor of the church!"

Sometimes we preachers need to remind ourselves of this calling on our lives. We sometimes need to rekindle the flame, as Paul told young Timothy (2 Tim. 1:6–7). Jeremiah said, "So the word of the Lord has brought me insult and reproach all day long. But if I say, 'I will not mention his word or speak in his name,' his word is in my heart like a fire, a fire shut up in my bones. I am weary of holding it in; indeed, I cannot" (Jer. 20:8–9). The calling to preach the gospel is inescapable. It is like "a fire shut up in my bones."

In addition to a conversion and a calling, we preachers need numerous other attributes: a love for God and a desire to know him, a genuine love for people, a passion for the lost, and a conviction about the importance of preaching. There is a dearth of God-called preachers and pastors in America at present. As a professor in a charismatic seminary, I am growingly alarmed at the shrinking number of graduates going into the pastorate in independent charismatic churches. Too often they have heard (or seen firsthand) the horror stories of churches running off pastors (an epidemic in our day) or pastors abusing their flocks. And yet, this calling can be supremely fulfilling. God has no plan B. He says to us, "Preach the word; be prepared in season and out of season; correct, rebuke and encourage—with great patience and careful instruction" (2 Tim. 4:2). But Jesus' example is instructive for all of us. Notice how his public ministry began.

First, we see him in the waters of the Jordan, being baptized by John the Baptist. Then, "Jesus, full of the Holy Spirit, left the Jordan and was led by the Spirit into the wilderness" (Luke 4:1). Mark's words are stronger here: "The Spirit immediately drove him out into the wilderness. And he was in the wilderness forty days, being tempted by Satan" (Mark 1:12 ESV). The words, "drove him out," translate the Greek, *ekballō*, which means literally "thrown out, cast out, or sent out by force." All effective ministry starts in the wilderness. John the Baptist was "a voice of one calling in the wilderness," and he "appeared in the wilderness, preaching a baptism of repentance for the forgiveness of sins" (Mark 1:3–4). But the results of Jesus' wilderness testings were that "Jesus returned to Galilee in the power of the Spirit" (Luke 4:14).

In the wilderness, without food or drink and bereft of any human companionship, Jesus reached the end of his natural resources, though not without angelic comfort. "He was with the wild animals, and angels attended him" (Mark 1:13). Only then did he return and launch his ministry. And so it is with us. Most dramatic breakthroughs in ministry are preceded by wilderness experiences. We're like batteries: God has to depower us before he can empower us. And seasons of fasting and prayer, humbling ourselves and repenting of sin, are almost guaranteed to bring blessing and fruitfulness in ministry. Notice, John "came preaching in the wilderness of Judea and saying, 'Repent, for the kingdom of heaven has come near'" (Matt. 3:1–2). Then came Jesus with the same message: "Repent and believe the good news" (Mark 1:15). And when Peter, having given the inaugural sermon as the church was launched on her worldwide mission at Pentecost, was asked by his hearers what they should do in response, he said, "Repent and be baptized" (Acts 2:38).

We always begin with repentance. We start low to go up high! Humble repentance and submission bring spiritual victory (James 4:6–10; 1 Peter 5:5–7). Only then comes intimacy with God and authentic spiritual empowerment. And God often uses the difficulties and demands of life to alert us to our sin and independence. So we should "endure hardship as discipline; God is treating you as his children. For what children are not disciplined by their father?" (Heb. 12:7). For the message of God's good news (which we advertise both with our lips and our lives) to get through, it must be communicated (preached) through sanctified and empowered lives.

But what was it that Jesus actually preached? Here is Mark's account: "Now after John was arrested, Jesus came into Galilee, preaching the gospel of God, and saying, 'The time is fulfilled, and the kingdom of God is at hand; repent, and believe in the gospel'" (Mark 1:14 RSV). First, it was *God's* gospel. We don't have the prerogative of altering that gospel, adding to it or subtracting from it. Nor do we have the right to substitute a different gospel. The gospel is not about a God who exists for our glory and pleasure, guaranteeing success, prosperity, and health, as too many preachers in America present it. Nor is it about funding Marxist revolutionaries in developing nations, as many in the liberal tradition would portray it. The gospel is about *the kingdom of God.* Jesus went about "preaching the gospel of the kingdom" (Matt. 4:23 RSV).

The gospel is not "fire insurance." It concerns the reign of God in our lives and on this earth. That is why the gospel is always accompanied with the call to repentance. We are quite happy, thank you, as fallen humanity to go our own independent way. If God would like to enhance our personal plans for happiness, fine. Otherwise, we generally are offended to be told that the real issue is sin and the only answer is Christ. As his body, we are called by Christ to make disciples, not merely converts. The gospel has to do with the totality of our lives, not just the so-called spiritual dimension. Inevitably, we come across as parochial. One God. One gospel. One Savior. Even though it is the best news anyone could ever hear, we will be hated and rejected for sharing it. "If the world hates you," Jesus said, "keep in mind that it hated me first" (John 15:18). People simply do not like to hear that they can come to God only on his terms. Jesus said, "I am the way and the truth and the life. No one comes to the Father except through me" (John 14:6). The way into the kingdom is the way of the cross.

"Jews demand signs," Paul wrote, "and Greeks look for wisdom, but we preach Christ crucified: a stumbling block to Jews and foolishness to Gentiles, but to those whom God has called, both Jews and Greeks, Christ the power of God and the wisdom of God" (1 Cor. 1:22–24). Here are the bullet points of the gospel (1 Cor. 15:3–8):

- Christ died for our sins according to the Scriptures.
- He was buried.
- He was raised on the third day according to the Scriptures.
- He appeared to [many].

I keep repeating these points throughout this volume because I have discovered that many Christians, even seminary students, are "fuzzy" on the gospel. Because it appeals neither to miracle-mongering nor prideful intellectualism, it is an offense. A crucified Messiah was an offense, literally scandalous, to the Jews of Paul's day. And the simple message of "Christ crucified" was moronic to the Gentiles.

Authentic preaching, then, will always center on the cross. The message we articulate and embody will always be cruciform.

Authentic preaching, then, will always center on the cross.

The gospel is at the heart of all ministry. When we meet together to worship, the gospel will always be our focal point. We will celebrate how the triune God reached down to rescue fallen humanity in the person of his Son. The old hymns of the faith would most often devote one verse each to the Father, the Son, and the Holy Spirit. As we worship at the table, we see the gospel proclaimed in the bread and cup. In more intimate gatherings in classrooms or living rooms, we will keep the gospel central. We will always be inclusive, welcoming those who have yet to embrace the Christ of the gospel. As we reach out as servants to hurting humanity—feeding the hungry, clothing the naked, visiting the sick and imprisoned, and advocating for the helpless—we will always do it with the name of Jesus on our lips, sharing the gospel as the opportunity presents itself.

Yes, there are both personal and social dimensions to the gospel. Problems arise, however, when we forget to preach the gospel as we move out in humble social service. Liberal Christians mobilized in the last century to alleviate the social ills of poverty, racism, classism, and sexism. (I often tell my students that our goal is to make all these "isms" to be "wasms"!) But the liberals lost the gospel of the crucified and risen Christ in the process and foundered. Toward the end of the last century, conservatives became socially and politically active on other issues, such as prayer in school, abortion, and pornography, but they also forgot the gospel and its sole power to transform lives. Years later they found the country as bad morally (or worse) as when they began. Only the gospel "is the power of God that brings salvation to everyone who believes" (Rom. 1:16).

Our message on the surface seems foolish and irrelevant to lost humanity, which is more likely to look to education, scientific technology, or even the government to solve all our problems. "Since the world in all its fancy wisdom never had a clue when it came to knowing God, God in his wisdom took delight in using what the world considered dumb—*preaching*, of all things!—to bring those who trust in him into the way of salvation" (1 Cor. 1:21 *THE MESSAGE*). Karl Barth, probably the most influential theologian of the twentieth century, loved to preach because he believed, based on the Bible's own testimony, that *God speaks* when the gospel is preached. "The gospel is an announcement, not about what we are to do for God, but about what He has done for us."[3] That wonderful story of Jesus and his love continually transforms us and motivates us to share this good news of saving grace with others.

The gospel enlivens our worship, prayer, witness, and service. That's why we need gospel preaching in our pulpits once again. In hearing the gospel and accepting Christ's invitation to his table, we are changed by God himself. God speaks to us through gospel preaching and invites us to his banquet in the Lord's Supper. It's all about what *he* is doing, not what we are doing.[4] "Pastors and teachers are not cruise directors who provide venues for everyone to channel all of their gifts and energies to the church, but they are deliverers of the message of Christ."[5] There is nothing more central than the gospel. There is nothing "deeper" than the gospel.

I cannot count the times that I have heard my charismatic friends speak as if gospel preaching is surface and that they are interested in "deeper" spiritual truths. I announced one time in an elders meeting of a charismatic church I was pastoring that I wanted to preach through the book of Romans. I noted that when I was Chaplain of the University at Oral Roberts University, I had preached through the first eight chapters of Romans with a tremendous response. (I still get letters expressing appreciation for that series, some thirty years later!). So I told the elders that I felt it was time to take our congregation on a journey through Romans. One of the elders spoke up quickly and vociferously, "If you do that, you'll kill the church!" I was speechless. Perhaps the primary reason that the charismatic movement is declining is because

---

3   J. D. Greear, Gospel: *Recovering the Power that Made Christianity Revolutionary* (Nashville: B & H, 2011),

4   See Michael Horton, *Christless Christianity: The Alternative Gospel of the American Church* (Grand Rapids: Baker, 2008), 218.

5   Horton, *Christless Christianity*, 229.

it has lost the gospel. God's good news is a bottomless, pristine pure lake of eternal truth. It is wondrous! You should be forever thankful for "those who have preached the gospel to you by the Holy Spirit sent from heaven. Even angels long to look into these things" (1 Peter 1:12). That's *deep!*

There has been a renewed appreciation in our day for the life and ministry of the martyred Lutheran pastor and theologian, Dietrich Bonhoeffer. What many have not learned, however, is how much Bonhoeffer valued preaching. Eberhard Bethge relates:

> Bonhoeffer loved to preach. When he found out that a relative of his might have a few months to live, he wrote, "What would I do if I learned that in four to six months my life would reach the end? I believe I would still try to teach theology as I once did and *to preach often.*[6]

At the very end, Bonhoeffer held a little service for his fellow prisoners in the small schoolroom where they were being held. He led in prayer, then shared the scriptures for the day, Isaiah 53:5 and 1 Peter 1:3. Then he gave an exposition of these wonderful gospel passages. Someone who was there provided this report of what happened next:

> He had hardly finished his last prayer when the door opened and two evil-looking men in civilian clothes came in and said: "Prisoner Bonhoeffer. Get ready to come with us." Those words "Come with us"—for all the prisoners they had come to mean one thing only—the scaffold. We bade him good-

---

6 Dietrich Bonhoeffer, *Gesammelte Schriften*, ed. Eberhard Bethge, 4 vols. (Munich: Chr. Kaiser Verlag, 1961), 4:7; cited in Clyde E. Fant, Jr. and William M. Pinson, Jr. (eds.), *20 Centuries of Great Preaching: An Encyclopedia of Preaching*, vol. 12 (Waco: Word, 1971), 105.

CHRISTIANITY IN **3D** 143

bye—he drew me aside—"This is the end," he said. "For me the beginning of life."[7]

One of the most popular professors in the seminary I attended always said he wanted to be preaching the gospel when the Lord called him home. He was doing just that one Sunday morning as a guest speaker in a Baptist church when, in the middle of his message, he suddenly slumped over and went to heaven. It was a little disconcerting for his hearers—but a glorious homegoing for this great gospel preacher!

Jesus was the master preacher. And we all, in one way or another, are purveyors of God's good news. Jesus taught, preached, and healed (Matt. 4:23; 9:35)—and so must we in the myriad ways he has called us to do so. We have explored the ministries of teaching and preaching. Now it's time to examine perhaps the most controversial ministry of all in our day—healing.

---

7 S. Payne Best, The Venlo Incident (Watford, Herts: Hutchinson, 1950), 200; cited in Eric Metaxas, *Bonhoeffer: Pastor, Martyr, Prophet, Spy* (Nashville: Thomas Nelson, 2010), 528.

CHAPTER NINE
HEALING

Both Jesus' message and ministry were centered on the kingdom of God. The parables alone reveal a teacher and preacher who was obsessed with the kingdom. And when the days came for him to begin his public ministry, both his forerunner, John the Baptist, and Jesus announced the kingdom with identical words: "Repent, for the kingdom of heaven has come near" (Matt. 3:1; 4:17). But the kingdom Jesus preached and embodied was unique. It was a kingdom of *love*. It was about loving God with your whole being and loving your neighbor as yourself (Mark 12:29–31). This was a radical love that extended even to one's enemies: "Love your enemies, do good to those who hate you, bless those who curse you, pray for those who mistreat you" (Luke 6:27). The messianic expectations of Jesus' day were more along the lines of a military *defeat* of their enemies and a political kingdom.

But Jesus declared right at the outset, in his hometown synagogue, that he was the fulfillment of Isaiah's prediction of a servant Messiah who would "proclaim good news to the poor. He has sent me to proclaim freedom for the prisoners and recovery of sight for the blind, to set the oppressed free, to proclaim the year of the Lord's favor" (Luke 4:18–19; Isa. 61:1–2). And he proceeded to do just that: The New Testament records almost two dozen healings and exorcisms, nine miracles demonstrating his power over nature, and three raisings of the dead.[1]

---

1   See the helpful chart in *The NIV Study Bible* (Grand Rapids: Zondervan, 2011), 1765.

"God anointed Jesus of Nazareth with the Holy Spirit," Peter would explain at Cornelius's house, "and he went around doing good and healing all who were under the power of the devil, because God was with him" (Acts 10:38). Jesus' kingdom was a spiritual kingdom, bringing the reign of God, with healing and deliverance for the people.

> Jesus' kingdom was a spiritual kingdom, bringing the reign of God, with healing and deliverance for the people.

John the Baptist couched his depiction of Jesus' end time ministry in spiritual terms as a Spirit-and-fire baptism (Luke 3:16). But after months of imprisonment, John was told about all these miracles of Jesus, and sent two of his disciples to ask, "Are you the one who is to come, or should we expect someone else?" (Luke 7:19):

> At that very time Jesus cured many who had diseases, sicknesses and evil spirits, and gave sight to many who were blind. So he replied to the messengers, "Go back and report to John what you have seen and heard: The blind receive sight, the lame walk, those who have leprosy are cleansed, the deaf hear, the dead are raised, and the good news is proclaimed to the poor. Blessed is anyone who does not stumble on account of me (vv. 21–23).

Later, Jesus sent out the seventy-two, saying, "Heal the sick who are there and tell them, 'The kingdom of God has come near to you'" (Luke 10:9). And when Jesus was accused of driving out demons by the power of Satan, he replied, "But if I drive out demons by the finger of God [see Ex. 8:19; 31:18 and Deut. 9:10], then the kingdom of God has come upon you" (Luke 11:20). So Jesus' miracles were signs of the kingdom, and we are forced to expand our categories for the salvation he offers us. *3D Christianity embraces the liberating truth that there are dimensions to our salvation that are mind boggling!*

First, our salvation is a process involving past, present, and future. I "have been saved" (Eph. 2:8); I am "being saved" (1 Cor.1:18); and I "will be saved" (Rom. 5:9). "Our salvation is nearer now than when we first believed" (Rom. 13:11). Second, we can already see that Christ came to save the

> 3D Christianity embraces the liberating truth that there are dimensions to our salvation that are mind boggling!

whole person. Jesus told a sick woman who had been healed by touching his cloak, "Daughter, your faith has saved you. Go in peace and be cured of your affliction" (Mark 5:34 NAB). Healing is a part of our salvation. Our bodies are so important to God that he is going to resurrect them! Earlier, at Capernaum, Jesus said two wonderful things to a paralyzed man who had been brought to him: "Son, your sins are forgiven" and "I tell you, get up, take your mat and go home," demonstrating that he had authority to forgive sins (Mark 2:1–12). But our salvation is even larger than that!

One day every knee will bow and every tongue confess "that Jesus Christ is Lord, to the glory of God the Father" (Phil. 2:10–11). Think of it! All people—small and great, known and unknown—will acknowledge with all the saints of all the ages, that Jesus is Lord! But our salvation doesn't stop even there. One day there will be "a new heaven and a new earth" (Rev. 21:1; Isa. 65:17). What a tragedy for anyone to spurn Christ and miss out on all these personal and cosmic blessings!

When Jesus sent out the Twelve, "he gave them power and authority to drive out all demons and to cure diseases, and he sent them out to proclaim the kingdom of God and to heal the sick" (Luke 9:1–2). And the book of Acts documents that this sort of ministry continued in the early church. In fact, this sort of ministry continued, albeit in a diminished scope, down the centuries in the church. About one-half to three-quarters of the way through the patristic period (the first five centuries), healing dropped off dramatically, and so did the growth and vitality of the church. Francis MacNutt has documented this and given us a clarion call to return to our biblical and historical roots.[2]

Healing and forgiveness of sins ought to be a part of "business as usual" in the church. Here is how James, the brother of our Lord, described it:

> Is anyone among you in trouble? Let them pray. Is anyone happy? Let them sing songs of praise. Is anyone among you sick? Let them call the elders of the church to pray over them and anoint them with oil in the name of the Lord. And the prayer offered in faith will make the sick person well; the Lord will raise them up. If they have sinned, they will be forgiven. Therefore confess your sins to each other and pray for each other so that you may be healed. The prayer of a righteous person is powerful and effective (James 5:13–16).

Notice that the spiritual and the physical are linked in this counsel. The wholeness we need encompasses both. We are a psychosomatic whole—multi-dimensional, if you will—and what affects one aspect of our nature affects, in one way or another, our whole being. Therefore, our approach to healing must be informed by this reality.

I serve in a university whose whole vision is based on this insight. Our goal has been to send out healers into every segment of society—into the whole world and into every person's world. Professionally trained graduates bring healing into the business world, educational world, the medical field, the religious world, and the arts and sciences. A pastor might find himself laying hands on the sick for their healing, while a counselor or psychiatrist would never physically touch her clients, but

---

2 Francis MacNutt, *The Healing Reawakening: Reclaiming Our Lost Inheritance* (Grand Rapids: Chosen, 2005).

would bring healing through other means. As believers we can continue Christ's ministry of teaching, preaching, and healing. "In traditional terms Jesus saves us from personal sin and from the effects of original sin which include ignorance, weakness of will, disoriented emotions, physical illness and death."[3]

But biblically, as we have already seen, healing extends from the personal to the societal. Persons suffer under unjust and unhealthy social structures that must be challenged and changed. That process in itself brings healing. 3D Christianity addresses not only the physical, mental, emotional, and spiritual dimensions, but also the relational, familial, financial, and political dimensions. Christianity was never meant to be merely a private, parochial enterprise, safely ensconced in its own little ghetto. We are called to be salt and light (Matt. 5:13–16). The church is the kingdom in miniature. It was meant to model kingdom values and goals. It is created by the kingdom and is the instrument of the kingdom.

Reading the New Testament broadly and carefully, one notices an interesting pattern when comparing Jesus' message with that of the early church. Whereas Jesus spoke incessantly about the kingdom, the church spoke more about the Spirit.[4] The reason this was so becomes clear upon reflection.

> The kingdom is wherever the Spirit is moving, convicting, saving, and healing.

The kingdom is wherever the Spirit is moving, convicting, saving, and healing. The Spirit himself brings the reign of God to humanity. The church is the instrument of the kingdom as she submits to the executive direction of the Spirit and moves in the wisdom and power of the Spirit. When Jesus brought kingdom power to bear against the demonic, ironically his opponents accredited his abilities to the demonic. He then quickly cautioned them against blaspheming the Spirit (Mark

---

3   Francis MacNutt, *Healing* (Notre Dame: Ave Maria Press, 1974), 49.
4   James D. G. Dunn, "Spirit and Kingdom," *Expository Times,* 82, 1970-71, 36-40.

3:22–29). This often goes unnoticed. Rejecting the gracious move of the Holy Spirit is "an eternal sin" (v. 29). There is no help or hope for that person. Therefore, what we are about as followers of Christ is of limitless significance for both time and eternity. No one else has these answers or offers this hope.

Every Christian tradition at its best has offered this kingdom hope and administered this natural and supernatural healing to humanity. The Roman Catholic Church, for example, never lost the healing dimension. So when the charismatic renewal emerged, the church simply baptized the movement into the church and gave it theological and pastoral guidance. Unfortunately, my own mother church, the Southern Baptist Convention, was unable to do so. Instead, strife and factions seemed to be the order of the day. This was a tragic development, given her historical roots. Records of Baptist life in colonial America reveal a Pentecostal/charismatic like Christianity—a 3D Christianity, if you will—that she later largely lost. The same is true for the Methodist tradition. We all need to get back to our roots!

Evangelicals in general share these roots, though many are unaware of this fact. Charles Spurgeon, for example, had a strong and well-known healing ministry, which biographies of his day documented. Unfortunately, the biographies of our day have excised this material. Spurgeon's parishioners—and there were many of them; he was the first megachurch pastor!—knew that if they were sick, all they needed was to get Spurgeon to pray for them and they would be healed.

Carl F. H. Henry was called by many the dean of evangelical theologians in the past century. What many do not know is that his pilgrimage began with a supernatural healing. Shortly after his conversion, he was stricken with acute appendicitis, from which he was healed through the prayers of the saints. He consulted closely with medical help and knew they were a part of God's gracious provision.

But I knew something more, that the great God who is sometimes glorified by the courageous and victorious bearing of one's thorn in the flesh is, on other occasions, equally glorified in the direct healing of the body no less than of the soul. I left for college in good time, reassured that God would and could supply every need.[5]

Instead of having his educational plans disrupted by this medical emergency, he received through prayer an instant, permanent healing, documented by his doctor.

I first saw the healing power of God in operation in the lives of my relatives. They were Pentecostals, Aunt Lue and Uncle Wilbur. Lou was my mom's twin sister. I saw these two radiant believers healed of everything imaginable, including, in Lou's case, a broken leg! Wilbur ran the tram that brought workers in and out of the potash mines near Carlsbad, New Mexico. He witnessed to every new worker that came on the job. There was one particular worker, however, with whom he had not had the chance to share his faith. At noon one day, Wilbur received an emergency call from inside the mine: "Wilbur, come quickly!" When he arrived, he saw a horrendous scene. The worker had sat down on the track with a ten-cup of water in his hand, and leaned back into a high-voltage wire. He was electrocuted, lying there lifeless, with blood coming from eyes, ears, and mouth.

Wilbur asked, "Isn't anybody going to do anything?" The miners replied, "Wilbur, there's nothing to do. The man is dead. We just need to get him out of here." Wilbur said, "Of course there's something we can do." He gathered the man into the tram, holding him in his lap. As they ascended, he prayed that the Lord would give the man back his life so that Wilbur could witness to him. Then he noticed the man's eyeballs

---

5   Carl F. H. Henry, *Confessions of a Theologian: An Autobiography* (Waco: Word Books, 1986), 59. Henry's entire account of this event is quite moving.

moving under his eyelids. The man was taken to the hospital, where the doctors examined him carefully. They told him, "You shouldn't be alive, and even if you survived, your brain should be scrambled. But there's nothing wrong with you. Get out of here."

The next morning (Saturday), my aunt and uncle were on his doorstep to invite him to church. He opened the door and said, "You don't have to say a word. I'll be at your church tomorrow." He went to their little Assemblies of God church the next day and went forward to give his life to Christ. Later he was called to preach. And the only thing he has to show from his electrocution is a bald spot on the back of his head where the high-voltage wire burned the hair from his scalp.

My uncle, Bill Hart, flew in the lead plane on the D-Day invasion. He came back from the war thinking that perhaps God was calling him into the ministry. Later he decided that the Lord wanted him to be a lawyer. Over the decades, he had a powerful ministry as a lawyer—helping young people and families get their lives back together, leading people to Christ, and praying for people to be healed or filled with the Holy Spirit. On his death bed, a close friend, who was terminally ill herself, was brought into the hospital room by friends and family to see Bill. They had all agreed that Bill didn't need to be told of her need. When they entered the room, Bill motioned toward her to come to his bedside. He said, "Come here. I want to pray for your healing." How did he know? God let him know. Bill's son, my cousin Steve Hart, is an episcopal priest in New York who has had a healing ministry for years. In fact, he has done numerous healing seminars together with Francis MacNutt, teaching other Christians how to pray for the sick.

My own parents went to be with the Lord within four days of each other in their eighties. Both were faithful witnesses to Christ, and dad was chairman of the deacons in our large Southern Baptist church for years. People came to me after my parents' deaths telling me story after story of how my parents would encourage and pray with them—even in a crowded mall.

I've also been blessed with many friends in the healing ministry. During seminary days, I met a very impressive, yet humble, servant of the Lord, a seminary peer named Randy Clark. Ultimately, Randy became a Vineyard pastor. God used him in a very dramatic way at the Airport Vineyard in Toronto in a historic meeting that led to the Toronto Revival movement. Randy told his fellow pastors, "We believe in healing and miracles in our church, but it's simply not happening." They all prayerfully humbled themselves before God, and God poured out his Spirit—and the rest is history! Randy has a truly global ministry in signs and wonders, teaching others to pray for the sick as well.

My wife and I had the privilege of planting a church in Louisville, Kentucky. We thought this would probably be our life's work together. Then one day Dr. Jimmy Buskirk called. Dr. Buskirk, a United Methodist, was the founding dean of the seminary at Oral Roberts University. He was inquiring of our interest in my teaching there. It took seven months of prayer and two trips to Tulsa to confirm our decision to go to Tulsa. Dr. Buskirk's winsome personality and dynamic testimony impressed us. He was serving as a young United Methodist pastor when he was diagnosed with an incurable disease of the retina. The doctors gave him no hope of saving his vision. He thought his ministry was over. But he wanted to keep all this a secret and do the best he could until that fateful denouement. He memorized the steps around the platform and practiced them in private. He listened to recordings of the Scriptures, memorized his texts, and held his Bible open—as if he were actually reading it—as he quoted the scripture by memory.

One Sunday morning, "Miss Virginia" came to him after the service and asked, "Jimmy, what's wrong with you?" Jimmy said, "Oh, Miss Virginia, I just have a cold." Miss Virginia and her elderly widow friends had a prayer group. She led the group in her exuberant and earthy ways. She replied to Dr. Buskirk, "Oh, hell, Jimmy! God wouldn't be waking me up in the middle of the night to pray for a cold." Jimmy was shocked and thought he would just shock her back. He said, "I'll tell you what's wrong, Miss Virginia. I'm losing my sight and losing my ministry." She retorted, "Not necessarily so! I'm going to be here right at this altar everyday [and she named a time], praying for your healing."

Sometimes Jimmy would peak into the room to check to see if she was keeping her word. And, sure enough, there she'd be. One day she noticed him peaking and said, "Come here. Let me pray for you." When she placed her hands on Dr. Buskirk's eyes, he felt a heat coming out of her hands. He grabbed her wrists, thinking she had been holding a hand warmer, and asked, "What did you do to me?" She asked, "What do you mean?" Then he told her about the intense heat coming out of her hands. Immediately, she began to clap her hands and rejoice, saying, "Jimmy, Jesus is healing you! Jesus is healing you!"

Dr. Buskirk returned to his ophthalmologist for a checkup. The doctor said, "You have better than 20/20 vision now. But you have a greater miracle than you realize. When I look at your retinas, they are *still* a mass of scars. You shouldn't be able to see at all!" When Dr. Buskirk told this story on the campus of ORU, Oral Roberts latched on to him and persisted until Jimmy accepted his invitation to become the founding dean of the seminary. And my wife, Thea, and I are glad he did!

Our present dean, Dr. Thomson Mathew, a Yale graduate, was a prayer chaplain at the City of Faith hospital Oral Roberts built. Dr. Mathew prayed for the first person admitted into the hospital and the last patient there when the hospital was closed. He also prayed for and with Oral Roberts himself. In a medical context the realities of healing are seen with crystal clarity. Either people are healed or they aren't. Wishful thinking simply won't cut it. And Oral Roberts himself was brutally honest about the process.

I remember a public healing service we had on campus where a person came out of their wheelchair and began to walk across the auditorium. People began to clap and shout in marvel. Oral went quickly to the microphone and told the audience that this person could already walk and that the doctor had simply recommended the wheelchair for her comfort. People have often said that Oral Roberts prayed for more people who have been healed than anyone who's ever lived—to which Oral would reply, "I've also prayed for more people who *haven't* been healed than anyone else. The older I get the fewer answers I have." He would often tell the story of praying for two twelve-year-old girls—both beautiful Christians, both completely blind. They stood in the same healing line at one of his crusades. One was completely and instantaneously healed. The other had nothing happen to her. And Oral would simply say, "I don't know why. God only knows."

When I was Chaplain of the University of ORU, I invited Joni Eareckson Tada to speak in a chapel service. Before the service, I said to her, "Joni, I've gained the impression from reading your books that you've decided that God simply doesn't want to heal you." She responded, "Absolutely not." Then she told me of a recent experience of praying with friends in a special season of fasting and prayer for healing. She said, "It is frustrating being married and unable to help my husband around the kitchen. People don't realize that when you're paralyzed that you have to become reconciled to your condition or simply lose your mind. It's not like seeking healing for a minor condition."

I told Joni, "You would love Oral's theology of healing. He says God always heals his own: Sometimes instantaneously, sometimes gradually, or sometimes ultimately at the resurrection. But God always heals his own." Joni replied, "I wish he would preach that more, because I have had to help some of my wheelchair-bound friends who haven't been healed at healing crusades pick up the pieces afterward."

That chapel service was surely one of the most powerful we've ever had. Joni is a radiant, powerful woman of faith. After her visit, I would often have one of our students in a wheelchair share their faith pilgrimage in chapel. For years I used to say, "If Billy would have more healing testimonies in his crusades and Oral would have more suffering testimonies in his crusades, then we might achieve the biblical balance on healing. This truth came through to me even more powerfully when my wife and I took a team of seven seminary students to Argentina.

We were guests of Omar Cabrera, who was the pastor of Vision de Futuro (Vision of the Future), a church of some 167,000 members. We saw astounding healing miracles. One day I said to Omar, "We talk about miracles a lot in America, but we don't see them the way you do here." Omar replied, "Perhaps one reason is that many of the people we reach out to have very little access to medical science. Either God heals them or they die." Then I asked, "Have you ever struggled with the question of why people are not healed." He replied quickly, "Absolutely! Some of the finest saints in the church have had accidents or illnesses and God hasn't healed them. Some have even died—and all this while miracles are happening almost daily around here." I said, "Do you have an answer for this?"

Again, Omar responded quickly, "Yes, I do." Omar would often go on extended personal retreats of fasting and prayer—"doing spiritual warfare," he called it—before his public crusades. So he decided to fast and pray to get an answer from God on why people sometimes are not healed. I asked, "And did God give you an answer?" Omar replied, "Yes. He told me, 'It's none of your business.'" Later I recalled that that was God's response to Job as well! No, not everyone we pray for is going to be healed. But does that mean we shouldn't pray for the sick? Is everyone we witness to saved? If not, should we quit sharing our faith? No, the more we pray and the more we share, the more positive results we will see.

Jesus Christ is still teaching, preaching, and healing today—*through us!* Our triune God is still the primary actor in the ongoing drama of redemption. There is simply no reason why we could not see

> Jesus Christ is still teaching, preaching, and healing today—
> *through us!*

revolutionary changes in church and society, if only we would desire and pursue God for his refreshing presence in our midst. Peter's words to his fellow Israelites in the temple precincts of Jerusalem at the beginning of his apostolic ministry possess an uncanny relevance to the church in America today: "Repent, then, and turn to God, so that your sins may be wiped out, that times of refreshing may come from the Lord" (Acts 3:19).

CONCLUSION

I've noticed that in recent days some of the most popular movies of the recent past are being brought back in 3D for a whole new audience. Perhaps Christianity needs to do the same! Younger generations of believers are leaving the church in droves, and many of the ones who stay seem more enamored with contemporary culture than with the historic faith of the church. The words of Jude, the brother of Jesus, carry tremendous contemporary relevance: "Dear friends, although I was very eager to write to you about the salvation we share, I felt compelled to write and urge you to contend for the faith that was once for all entrusted to God's holy people" (Jude 3). The inerrant Word of God and the eternal truths of the gospel and all its implications are under attack today as never before. We need to contend for the faith, "the sound doctrine that conforms to the gospel concerning the glory of the blessed God" (1 Tim. 1:10–11) as never before.

> We need a 3D Christianity, strongly rooted in a Trinitarian faith, fully surrendered to the work of the Holy Spirit, and mobilized in the saving, healing ministry of our Lord.

If ever America needed an awakening, it is today! We should pray to our sovereign Lord for a powerful new outpouring of the Holy Spirit, for liberating grace to get the church back on course. We need a 3D

Christianity, strongly rooted in a Trinitarian faith, fully surrendered to the work of the Holy Spirit, and mobilized in the saving, healing ministry of our Lord.

A seminary friend of mine grew up knowing Cliff Barrows and Billy Graham. Once he was with Dr. Graham in his home, and Billy held up his Bible and said, "Jim, if you want to be a man of God, know this Book, love this Book, believe this Book, preach this Book." Once as a teenager, I was riding in the front seat of a car that Oral Roberts was driving to a local high school, where he was scheduled to speak. I said, "Brother Roberts, I feel like my Southern Baptist church cheated me because they didn't teach me about the Holy Spirit." Oral Roberts replied, "Larry, be thankful for your background because they taught you to base your Christian walk on the Word of God and not on your feelings and experiences." He went on to add, "We Pentecostal young people had an experience at the altar on Sunday morning that we tried to live on all week long. You were taught the Word of God."

In effect, the primary purpose of this modest little volume was simply to highlight some of the most liberating, but too often neglected, truths of the Word of God. I have become increasingly alarmed at the lack of biblical and theological roots among the young people entering our Christian colleges today, especially charismatics. I have often observed a fervency of spirit, but combined with a rather relativistic mindset when it comes to the eternal truths of the gospel. The Bible itself has become the most neglected book on our bookshelves. I have often asked people in churches where I've preached, "How many of you believe everything you read in the newspaper?" Very few, if any, raise their hand. Then I ask, "How many of you believe everything you read in the Bible?" Usually, everyone raises their hand. Then I ask, "Then why do you spend more time most days reading something you can't always believe than you do something you can *always* believe?"

So put your 3D glasses on: Open the Bible and ask the Holy Spirit to reveal his liberating truth to you as never before. Draw close to your heavenly Father again. Surrender afresh to the Lordship of Christ in your life. Ask the Holy Spirit to fill you anew with his love and power. Cry out for a holy passion for the kingdom and a renewed compassion for lost and suffering humanity. God hears and answers such biblically based prayers. We could have a new Pentecost in America! So embrace and enjoy 3D Christianity—it is your heritage. And once you've entered into God's fullness, make it your legacy to future generations. "May the God of hope fill you with all joy and peace as you trust in him, so that you may overflow with hope by the power of the Holy Spirit" (Rom. 15:13).

CPSIA information can be obtained
at www.ICGtesting.com
Printed in the USA
LVHW080540120721
692416LV00011BB/1020